HOW TO MAKE BETTER DECISIONS

14 SMART TACTICS FOR CURBING YOUR BIASES, MANAGING YOUR EMOTIONS, AND MAKING FEARLESS DECISIONS IN EVERY AREA OF YOUR LIFE!

DAMON ZAHARIADES

ARTOFPRODUCTIVITY.COM

CONTENTS

PART III
**HOW TO OPTIMIZE YOUR DECISION-
MAKING RESULTS**

OTHER BOOKS BY DAMON ZAHARIADES

The Mental Toughness Handbook

The definitive, step-by-step guide to developing mental toughness! Exercises included!

To-Do List Formula

Finally! Discover how to create to-do lists that work!

The Art Of Saying NO

Are you fed up with people taking you for granted? Learn how to set boundaries, stand your ground, and inspire others' respect in the process!

The Procrastination Cure

Discover how to take quick action, make fast decisions, and finally overcome your inner procrastinator!

Fast Focus

Here's a proven system that'll help you to ignore distractions, develop laser-sharp focus, and skyrocket your productivity!

The 30-Day Productivity Plan

Need a daily action plan to boost your productivity? This 30-

day guide is the solution to your time management woes!

The 30-Day Productivity Plan - VOLUME II

30 MORE bad habits that are sabotaging your time management - and how to overcome them one day at a time!

The Time Chunking Method

It's one of the most popular time management strategies used today. Triple your productivity with this easy 10-step system.

80/20 Your Life!

Achieve more, create more, and enjoy more success. How to get more done with less effort and change your life in the process!

Small Habits Revolution

Change your habits to transform your life. Use this simple, effective strategy for adopting any new habit you desire!

Morning Makeover

Imagine waking up excited, energized, and full of self-confidence. Here's how to create morning routines that lead to explosive success!

The Joy Of Imperfection

Finally beat perfectionism, silence your inner critic, and overcome your fear of failure!

The P.R.I.M.E.R. Goal Setting Method

An elegant 6-step system for achieving extraordinary results in every area of your life!

Digital Detox

Disconnect to reconnect. Discover how to unplug and enjoy a more mindful, meaningful, and rewarding life!

For a complete list, please visit

http://artofproductivity.com/my-books/

YOUR FREE GIFT

~

As my way of saying thank you for purchasing *How to Make Better Decisions*, I'd like to offer you my 40-page action guide titled *Catapult Your Productivity! The Top 10 Habits You Must Develop to Get More Things Done.*

It's in PDF format, so you can print it out easily and read it at your leisure. This guide will show you how to develop core habits that'll help you to get more done in less time.

You can grab your copy by clicking on the following link and joining my mailing list:

http://artofproductivity.com/free-gift/

You'll also receive periodic tips for overcoming procrastination, developing effective morning routines, sharpening your focus, and more!

On that note, let's get started. We have a lot to cover. You'll find that *How to Make Better Decisions* is jam-packed with practical advice and exercises you can put to immediate use.

INTRODUCTION

 The choices we make dictate the life we lead.

— BILL RAGO IN *RENAISSANCE MAN*

M ost of us take decision-making for granted. We make choices without sufficiently evaluating the variables that impact the results of our choices. Oftentimes, we fail to recognize these variables, which causes us to make uninformed decisions. Our results are predictably less than stellar. We might even make things worse than had we not made a decision at all. The law of unintended consequences is more likely to affect us when we overlook (or outright ignore) important factors in the decision-making process.

We can improve our results by taking greater care with

how we make choices. If we do so methodically, considering every variable that might impact our results rather than trusting our intuition, we stand to achieve better outcomes.

Ultimately, it's possible to learn how to *consistently* make good decisions. This book will give you the tools you need to do so. We'll create simple, effective systems you can use to make logical decisions, quickly and with absolute confidence.

What to Expect in *How to Make Better Decisions*

In *PART I: Understanding Our Decision-Making Process*, we'll investigate how we make decisions, why we often make poor ones, and explore the obstacles that make us stumble. Here, we'll lay the foundation. Learning to make better decisions requires first examining our current processes. We'll highlight common bad habits and routines so we can replace them with more useful ones. We'll discuss the role of emotions, fake urgency, and our tendency to procrastinate. We'll also examine our propensity to make assumptions and cling to counterproductive biases.

In *PART II: 14 Tactics for Making Better Decisions*, we'll cover specific formulas for making good, informed decisions. This is the bulk of the book. It contains the most actionable content. Each chapter ends with a simple, practical exercise designed to help you apply what you've learned.

We'll conclude with *PART III: How to Optimize Your Deci-*

sion-Making Results. In this final section, we'll explore how to bring about the most favorable outcomes possible given your options. We'll talk about the questions you should ask yourself before making decisions. We'll also discuss the value of having a feedback loop in place and how to create one that works.

Business Decision-Making vs. Personal Decision-Making

Many of the systems and models described in this book are used today by today's business leaders. But note, they are just as effective in *personal* decision-making. This means you can apply them in your job, at home, or at school. You can use them when making decisions with friends, family, or colleagues.

Along these lines, many of these systems can be used in a collaborative setting with multiple actors providing data and opinions. This means you can easily include others into the decision-making process if you so desire. Having said that, this book focuses on *individual* decision-making, where *you* are the sole actor.

Two Quick Notes before We Begin

First, we're going to cover a lot of material in the following pages. But don't feel intimidated. We'll go through it together, step by step.

Second, while we'll spend ample time covering this

material, we're not going to *waste* time. You'll notice *How to Make Better Decisions* is a fast-moving book. There are no stories as you might find in other self-improvement books. There is no unnecessary investigation into psychology or scientific research. In other words, no padding. The purpose of this book is to provide the material you need in a no-nonsense manner and show you how to use it. *How to Make Better Decisions* is, above all else, an actionable book.

To that end, let's get started.

PART I

UNDERSTANDING OUR DECISION-MAKING PROCESS

~

We make hundreds, sometimes thousands, of choices each day. Most of them are small and inconsequential. Examples include those that concern what we'll eat, what we'll wear, and whether we should take a nap today or continue to peruse Facebook and Twitter. Experts claim we make over 200 decisions each day regarding food alone.[1]

Weightier decisions require greater care and assessment. These are the ones that carry larger consequences. Examples include quitting a job we hate, starting a family, leaving a toxic relationship, or finally buying that big-ticket item you've long dreamed of owning (sports car, large house, boat, etc.).

Before we can learn to make consistently good decisions, we need to evaluate how we currently make them. This section of *How to Make Better Decisions* will investigate the factors that influence our decision-making. Some of them are detrimental to the process and lead to undesirable outcomes. Highlighting them is the first step toward removing them from the process. Removing them will save us a lot of wasted time and avoidable regret down the road.

It's important that we accept responsibility for our decisions as well as the outcomes they produce. Admittedly, doing so is difficult when things turn out badly. If you're like me, you'll be tempted to absolve yourself of blame, chalking up undesirable outcomes as a result of misfortune rather than poor decision-making. But there's immense value in accepting responsibility. It reinforces the truth that we can exert massive control over our lives via our choices.

These are the reasons we must examine our current decision-making process. Let's dig in.

---

1. Sobal, Jeffery, Wansink, Brian (2007). "Mindless Eating: The 200 Daily Food Decisions We Overlook." *Environment and Behavior*. 39:1, 106-23, https://doi.org/10.1177/0013916506295573

HOW WE MAKE DECISIONS

 You cannot make progress without making decisions.

— JIM ROHN

W e like to think we make decisions logically. We imagine ourselves meticulously weighing our options and choosing the most rational one given our circumstances.

In reality, we tend to rely on our intuition and emotions in the moment. This is certainly the case when we make unimportant decisions that have minimal effect on our quality of life (e.g. what to eat). But we also do so when making decisions that carry greater consequences (e.g. starting a family). While emotions are unquestionably beneficial in most situations, they complicate the decision-making process.

The Role of Emotion in Decision-Making

Humans act with emotion. We think with emotion. We deliberate with emotion. Everything we do is done from an emotional perspective. This may seem counterproductive, but it's actually a welcome trait. We *need* emotion to live rewarding lives. So we should expect emotion to play a significant role when we make decisions. Emotion may seem like the antithesis of logic, and therefore an obstacle to our making rational choices, but it serves as a valuable guide.

Having said that, it's important to prevent our emotions from playing a dominant role in our decision-making. Allowing them to control the process makes us impulsive. This impulsiveness prompts us to make irrational choices that result in poor outcomes.

Our emotions may also paralyze us. If we allow them control, they can provoke fear and anxiety in the face of uncertainty. This leads to indecision, which can be just as harmful as making a terrible decision.

Our emotions also open the door to biases. Our personal feelings make us more inclined to consider some options and less inclined to consider others. These biases, which we'll cover in more detail later, wreak havoc with the decision-making process.

We shouldn't try to silence our emotions when we

make decisions. Emotion should play a role, particularly when our choices involve our values and convictions. However, we should remain aware of how our emotions can impede the decision-making process if they're allowed to drown out logic and reason.

The Role of Values in Decision-Making

Making good choices isn't just about obtaining sufficient information and methodically weighing our options. It also involves our personal and professional values. What do we stand for? What are the moral standards and principles that drive us? What type of person do we want to be?

These values inform our goals and give us purpose. Without them, we'd base our decisions on the easiest and quickest path toward success with no regard for whether we're acting with integrity.

For example, suppose you operate a small business. Sales are down. Profit is down. You're desperate to reverse the trend. If you ignore your values when considering your options, you risk making dubious choices that conflict with your core principles. The choices you make and the actions you ultimately take may indeed boost sales. They might result in greater profit. But you'll feel unsettled. You'll likely experience regret, guilt, and even shame.

When we allow our values to guide our decisions, we feel less troubled by the risks. Our choices, assuming they're properly informed, are accompanied by less stress and worry. Even when our results are disappointing, it's easier to accept them because we're acting in accordance with our personal and professional standards.

Does the inclusion of our values in the decision-making process complicate the process? Yes. Our values act as checks against our impulses. They restrict us, limiting our options. But they also ensure that our choices align with our convictions. Our values help us to make decisions we can take pride in, even when the outcomes are disheartening.

Weighing the Costs vs. the Benefits of Our Decisions

Every decision we make is a trade-off. We stand to gain something, but we also stand to lose something in the process. (In economic terms, this loss is referred to as an "opportunity cost.")

For example, suppose you're deciding what to eat for dinner. You've narrowed your options to a chicken salad and a pizza. If you choose the salad, you'll have to forego the pizza. If you choose the pizza, you'll have to sacrifice the salad (you could technically eat both, but you'd probably regret doing so).

Each option carries benefits. The salad is healthy. You'll feel good for eating it. On the other hand, pizza is delicious! Each option imposes a cost. Eating the salad means doing without the mouthwatering taste and flavor of pizza. Eating the pizza might mean abandoning your diet. It may even involve some gastrointestinal distress.

This trade-off is present in every decision we make,

from the trivial to the consequential. It's there when we choose between staying in a job we hate and looking for other career opportunities. It's there when we consider getting married or staying single. It's there when we decide whether to purchase a home in a particular city. To make good decisions that lead to favorable outcomes, we must recognize the existence of this trade-off. Only then can we identify and weigh the associated costs and benefits.

The goal, of course, is to maximize the benefits we enjoy from our decisions while minimizing their attendant costs. Unfortunately, the weighting process is sometimes troublesome. The costs and benefits that accompany our options are not always obvious to us. Discerning them requires careful investigation. The systems and tactics we'll cover in *Part II* of this book will prove invaluable for overcoming this struggle.

WHY WE MAKE POOR DECISIONS

" Good decisions come from experience. Experience comes from making bad decisions.

— Mark Twain

As noted, we like to believe that we consistently make good decisions. We imagine ourselves carefully weighing our options and choosing those that make the most sense given our circumstances and goals. After all, we're rational, reasoned human beings. Making bad decisions contradicts that persona.

The problem is, numerous obstacles stand in our way. They complicate the decision-making process and often cause us to make questionable choices that lead to regrettable outcomes.

In this section, we'll examine the most common obstacles. Once we've identified them and understand their influence, we can take steps to avoid and overcome them.

Unmanaged Emotions

We discussed emotions as they relate to decision-making in the previous section. They're essential to the process. Moreover, they're unavoidable. The important thing to remember is that our emotions are a double-edged sword when it comes to making decisions.

On the one hand, they help us to understand our present circumstances. Being aware of our emotional state makes us more aware of the stakes inherent in our choices. This awareness can spur us to make better-reasoned decisions.

On the other hand, if we fail to manage our emotions, they can cause us to become overly concerned with the potential for negative outcomes. We become fearful, focusing on threats and inflating their perceived impact rather than rationally analyzing the information we've obtained and logically weighing our options. When this happens, the decision-making process can deteriorate into a flight-or-fight response.

Our emotions can help us to make smart, reasoned choices. But we must properly manage our emotions to prevent them from commandeering the decision-making process and turning it into an exercise in self-preservation.

False Sense of Urgency

We often feel the need to *do something* rather than deliberate. We prioritize taking action over contemplation.

Sometimes, there exists true urgency. External factors compel us to make quick decisions. Deadlines loom and imply grave consequences for inaction and indecision.

Other times, this feeling of urgency is a false one. It stems from impatience, an impulse toward busyness, and a mistaken correlation between said busyness and productivity and progress. Some folks try to *manufacture* a false sense of urgency to motivate themselves and others to take action. They feel this trumped-up urgency overcomes complacency.

The problem is, while false urgency can pressure us to be more decisive, it can also cause us to make terrible choices. In our haste to decide, we risk overlooking pertinent information and valid options. This bogus need for speed may also spur us to disregard or quash conflicting information or dissenting opinions (when we involve others in the decision-making process).

To be sure, some decisions are time-sensitive. They require prompt action. But when there is no reason to act immediately, we should take the time we need to consider the relevant variables and thoroughly evaluate our options.

Lack of Urgency (Procrastination)

This is the opposite of false urgency. But it can be just as detrimental to the decision-making process.

Lack of urgency tempts us to procrastinate. After all, why hurry the process if doing so is unnecessary? As noted above, we should resist fabricating urgency to compel decisiveness. But it's also important that we recognize the dangers inherent in procrastinating our decisions.

Procrastination is an emotional response to our circumstances. The decision (or action) in front of us makes us feel bad in some way. Perhaps it bores us, makes us anxious, or causes us to doubt our skills, knowledge, and expertise. Perhaps we feel the decision is too difficult to make given all of the information and variables that must be considered to make a well-reasoned choice.

Procrastination is especially problematic because it is often accompanied by other negative emotions, such as fear, guilt, low self-esteem, and even shame. These feelings impose significant obstacles in the decision-making process. They invariably lead to indecisiveness. This mental state impedes our ability to make decisions that ultimately produce our desired outcomes.

Procrastinating isn't *always* harmful to the decision-making process. In fact, it can occasionally have a positive effect. Delaying the process may allow outstanding issues to resolve themselves (or at least become less consequential). Additionally, doing so can expand our available options, some of which may prove to be better than those previously under consideration.

Having said this, a lack of urgency typically carries consequences. Procrastinating decisions sets the stage for unrealized goals, missed opportunities, and deliberation that takes much longer and consumes more attentional resources than necessary.

Overoptimism

Most people are naturally optimistic. Sure, each of us know a few habitual complainers and killjoys. But most of us believe we're unlikely to experience negative events. This is called optimism bias.

This predisposition can have a positive effect on our decision-making. The more optimistic we feel regarding the prospective results of our decisions, the more empowered we feel to *make* decisions. Fear and anxiety have a weaker hold on us, lowering our susceptibility to indecision in the face of uncertainty.

That said, overoptimism imposes serious potential consequences. It encourages us to rush into decisions. We underestimate the risks involved with our choices because we anticipate results that are more favorable than reality suggests.

For example, suppose you're considering opening a restaurant. You've long dreamed of doing so and are naturally excited by the prospect. Overoptimism may cause you to overlook that previous businesses have failed in the location you've chosen. It might encourage you to dismiss the enormous startup costs involved in the endeavor. It may blind you to the fact that 80 percent of new restaurants fail within five years of opening.

Ultimately, unchecked optimism leads to making less accurate decisions. It causes us to forge ahead without sufficiently evaluating the information, options, and risks that are pertinent to our decisions.

Loss Aversion

We obviously like to acquire things we value. But we absolutely *hate* to lose things we value. For example, consider an outfit you purchased long ago but have never worn. Buying it gave you a sense of satisfaction. It made you feel good. Now imagine how you'd feel discarding the outfit. You've never worn it, so discarding it shouldn't have a huge impact on your wardrobe options. But you'll still be highly resistant to throwing it out (or giving it away).

Your feelings over the potential loss of the item are amplified when compared to your feelings regarding its acquisition. Cognitive psychologists and behavioral economists call this loss aversion.

Loss aversion hamstrings our ability to make well-reasoned decisions. Our fear of losing something we value causes us to be unduly wary.

For instance, suppose you're considering investing $100,000. But the idea of investing in stocks (or even mutual funds) fills you with dread. Weighing the potential *loss* of your money more heavily than the potential reward (capital appreciation, dividends, etc.) leads you to put the money into a savings account. It's an overcautious decision that stifles your return on investment.

Concern Regarding Our Public Image

We care about others' perception of us. We want our friends, peers, business partners, and acquaintances to think we're smart, resourceful, and successful. This is a natural tendency. The problem is, left unchecked it can reach the level of obsession. That's the point at which it can adversely impact our decisions.

When we become overly concerned with how others perceive us, we start to make decisions based on their implicit (or even *imagined*) approval. This inclination handicaps the decision-making process. It prompts us to dismiss reasonable, even preferable, options because they fail to align with others' opinions. In some cases, it may even prevent us from making a decision we know to be in our best interest.

For example, suppose you're thinking about leaving a toxic relationship. You're convinced that doing so is the right decision. But your friends constantly praise your partner's intelligence, wit, compassion, and honesty. They're unaware of the toxicity because you prefer privacy and have thus chosen not to disclose the true circumstances. In this case, your friends' praise of your partner may dissuade you from making the decision you feel is the correct one.

You might be overly concerned with their perception of your decision, despite their lacking the relevant details.

And so you hesitate. You doubt yourself. You may even convince yourself the decision you previously knew to be correct is a poor one.

Anxiety regarding how others think of us impedes our ability to make wise choices. We second guess ourselves and often end up choosing options that align with others' opinions rather than our interests.

Coming up Next...

Cognitive biases are among the most prominent roadblocks to the decision-making process. The next chapter is devoted to examining the ten most detrimental when it comes to making smart choices.

It's a fairly long chapter. But I encourage you to stick with it. The discussion moves quickly and offers insight into some of the most common and dangerous decision-making mistakes. It also provides actionable tips for over-coming each of them. The following chapter sets much of the foundation for *Part II: 14 Tactics for Making Better Decisions.*

10 COGNITIVE BIASES THAT IMPACT OUR DECISIONS

" Ninety percent of all mental errors are in your head.

— YOGI BERRA

Cognitive biases are mental shortcuts. They help us to simplify, process, and interpret information. On the one hand, they serve a useful purpose. We're constantly inundated with information throughout the day. Our brain creates these biases to make sense of it all. They allow us to filter through the information, identify what is important to us, and use that insight to make decisions.

That's the ideal scenario.

In practice, our cognitive biases often distort our

perception of reality. They prompt us to make hasty, reckless and erroneous judgments, which in turn cause us to make terrible decisions.

These biases also lead to blind spots. We fail to recognize our imprudence, believing ourselves to be rational when, in truth, we entertain preconceived notions stemming from logical fallacies. In this way, these "mental shortcuts" pose as mental *errors* that can completely derail the decision-making process.

All of us harbor cognitive biases. And all of us repeatedly fall victim to them. It's part of our nature. But this doesn't mean we must surrender to them. On the contrary, outsmarting our biases is crucial to our ability to make well-reasoned decisions. To this end, we'll examine the 10 most common, counterproductive cognitive biases below. You'll no doubt be familiar with many of them. But a few may surprise you.

#1 - Anchoring Bias

Whenever we're faced with multiple options, our brain tries to create an "anchor." This anchor is usually the first bit of information we learn about our circumstances. It serves as a reference point by which we compare and judge each option.

For example, suppose you intend to buy a car. You visit a dealership and are approached by a salesperson. This individual, after hearing your budget, shows you a model that is *above* your budget. The salesperson is creating an anchoring price (rather than allowing your brain to do it). The intent is not to persuade you to purchase this more expensive car, but to make lower-priced vehicles seem reasonable by comparison. By doing so, the salesperson can reduce your resistance to making a purchase.

Anchoring bias is occasionally useful as it helps us to filter information. We can quickly sift through a mountain of details that might otherwise overwhelm us.

But in most cases, this bias hurts the decision-making process. It makes us susceptible to tunnel vision whereby we ignore or misinterpret relevant information and make irrational assumptions.

HOW TO OVERCOME IT: This bias is particularly difficult to defeat. But even if we can't eliminate it, we can significantly reduce its influence on our judgment and choices. First, acknowledge the anchor established by your brain. Recognize that its relevance is probably tangential, at best.

Second, replace this subconsciously-set anchor with an anchor of your choosing. Doing so allows you to establish an anchor that is more directly related to your needs and goals.

#2 - Confirmation Bias

This bias is arguably the most widely recognized one among the lot. Most people have heard of it. And because it's so pervasive, most of us regularly succumb to it.

Confirmation bias arises from our preconceived beliefs and opinions. We overvalue information that aligns with these beliefs and opinions and undervalue information that detracts from them.

For example, suppose you're reading an article about government spending. If you're like most people, you have an opinion regarding how the government should spend money. If the article presents information that corroborates your opinion, you're more likely to embrace it. If the article presents information that challenges or refutes your opinion, you're more likely to dismiss it.

This shouldn't cause shame. All of us struggle with confirmation bias because it happens on a subliminal, almost instinctive level. That said, it's important to recognize that it distorts our perception of facts and details, and can cause us to make lamentable choices. It can even cause us to treat others unfairly if they entertain beliefs and opinions that vary from our own.

HOW TO OVERCOME IT: First, challenge your opinions. Ask yourself what informs them. Why do you hold them? Are they based on data or emotions?

Second, venture outside any echo chamber relevant to the decision in front of you. It's easy to become ensnared in such echo chambers, especially on social media. If you can extricate yourself from them, you'll be less susceptible to the prevailing viewpoints and better able to make reasoned, well-informed choices.

Third, discuss your decision with those who hold opinions that differ from your own. Here, you're not trying to decide by committee. Rather, you're exploring dissenting viewpoints that challenge your preconceived notions.

#3 - Availability Bias

This bias assigns greater gravity to information that comes to mind quickly than information that doesn't. Our brain assumes that something that can be immediately recalled must be important, and everything else must be decidedly less so.

The availability bias, also known as the availability heuristic, is a mental shortcut. It allows us to process information quickly when we lack the resources or willingness to conduct a full investigation. It springs into action when we must make a decision or judgment but have little time to consider every relevant factor. Unfortunately, it can also lead to errors in our thinking. These errors can cause us to make regrettable decisions.

For example, suppose you're considering purchasing a new vehicle. Your current vehicle is on its last legs and needs to be replaced. Let's further suppose that recent news reports have focused on a rising national unemployment rate. Each night, you hear about people losing their jobs. These reports cause you to consider the prospect of losing your own job. Consequently, you decide to postpone purchasing a new vehicle.

This might be a good decision if your job is truly at

risk. But it's likely the availability bias, arising from the barrage of distressing employment news, is distorting your perspective. If your job is not at risk, the decision to postpone replacing your failing vehicle is a poor one.

This bias is problematic because it spurs us to make decisions based on incomplete, and thus misleading, information. Just because we can immediately recall particular details doesn't make those details relevant and reliable.

HOW TO OVERCOME IT: Controlling this bias requires two things that work in tandem. First, we must possess enough self-awareness to recognize that the information we immediately recall when faced with a decision is almost certainly inadequate on its own. So we should question it. We should ask ourselves, *"Is this information as reliable as it seems on the surface?"*

Second, we must commit to a more deliberative inquiry into factors that are less obvious, and thus come to mind less quickly. Such factors are often just as impactful to our decisions. Overlooking them can even prove disastrous.

#4 - Optimism Bias

Optimism is good. Research suggests that people who have a positive outlook are more likely to be happier, more likely to achieve their goals, and more open to new ideas and experiences. Having said that, overoptimism can skew our frame of mind when we make decisions.

Optimism bias leads us to believe we're less susceptible to unfavorable outcomes than suggested by our circumstances. We can accept that bad things may happen to others, but not to us. This unrealistic perspective makes us overly confident in our knowledge, abilities, and level of control in any given situation. Meanwhile, it causes us to overlook, and even dismiss, information that would otherwise prove useful in the decision-making process.

For example, suppose you're thinking of creating an emergency fund. This fund would be available in the event you lose your job, suffer a costly health issue, or face any type of financial distress. The optimism bias might convince you that you're in less danger of such circumstances than is truly the case. Encouraged by an overly cheery outlook, you may decide to put less money into your emergency fund or decide against creating one altogether. Such decisions can leave you wholly unprepared if financial calamity strikes.

Entertaining a "glass is half full" outlook is beneficial in many ways, some of which are mentioned above. But it can also serve as our Achilles heel, causing us to be unrealistic about our circumstances and unreasonable when making important decisions.

How to overcome it: We can use two cognitive "tricks" to counteract the optimism bias. First, we can adopt an outsider's view of our circumstances. Doing so lessens the influence of our natural, overly-rosy assumptions regarding our knowledge, abilities, and level of control. It forces us to rely instead on objective data.

Second, we can view a decision in terms of what might go wrong. Here, we imagine undesirable outcomes stemming directly from our choices. Once we've done so, we work backwards to determine what went wrong. Psychologist and author Daniel Kahneman refers to this strategy as taking a "postmortem approach" to decision-making. It short circuits our overconfidence.

#5 - Dunning-Kruger Effect

This bias encourages us to believe we're more competent than is actually the case in a given situation. We trust that we're smart enough, capable enough, and sufficiently informed to proceed when, in fact, we are not.

The Dunning-Kruger effect is based on research conducted by psychologists David Dunning and Justin Kruger. They found that people who entertain this bias overestimate their capabilities and knowledge and lack adequate self-awareness to recognize the error. Consequently, these individuals believe they fully understand their circumstances when closer scrutiny would reveal their overconfidence.

All of us are susceptible to this cognitive bias. In fact, all of us have likely fallen victim to it at some point. Some of us, myself included, routinely do so.

For example, I might decide to visit a new restaurant and assume I know how to find it. This assumption overestimates my knowledge, and encourages me to head out without directions or the restaurant's address.

Or imagine yourself at your job. You're eager to impress your boss because doing so might lead to a promotion and higher salary. So, when offered a large project, you enthusiastically take it on assuming you possess the skills and knowledge to see it through completion. Then, reality sets in and you slowly realize that you're lacking in both in key areas. You've fallen prey to the Dunning-Kruger effect.

Again, this happens to all of us at some point. And because this bias can have disastrous results, it's important that we learn to control it.

HOW TO OVERCOME IT: The key to outsmarting this bias is to develop enough self-awareness to recognize we're always susceptible to it. This self-awareness discourages overconfidence. Rather than assuming we're familiar with, and competent in, a given situation, we instinctively look for our blindspots. We *assume* they exist.

Another useful practice is to regularly solicit feedback from others, particularly those who are proficient in our areas of interest. Constructive criticism will often uncover a lack of insight or expertise. This information is valuable because it gives us an opportunity to recognize and remedy troublesome blindspots and oversights.

#6 - Loss Aversion Bias

We discussed the broad strokes of loss aversion bias in the previous chapter. I won't rehash those points here. But this bias deserves more attention, particularly with regard to recognizing its influence on our decisions and ultimately overcoming it.

Loss aversion bias often discourages us from making decisions altogether. Every choice is accompanied by a risk of loss, even if that loss manifests merely as an opportunity cost (e.g. choosing option A precludes choosing option B). This is the reason companies offer trial periods during which we can use their products without paying for them. They remove the potential for loss, thereby encouraging us to make a decision.

Loss aversion bias can also dissuade us from taking calculated, reasoned risks. For example, we might decline to take on important projects at our jobs due to the attendant visibility. We may avoid purchasing a new home, afraid it'll turn into a money pit. We might forgo the opportunity to start a side business, concerned we'll be left with little time to spend with family and friends.

In each of these cases, the prospect of losing something we value (our reputation at work, our savings, or our social life) prompts us to reject taking sensible risks. Our fear of loss prompts us to play it safe, even though doing so causes us to miss out on promising opportunities.

. . .

HOW TO OVERCOME IT: Two tactics are effective toward controlling this bias. First, we should frame every decision in terms of its accompanying risks and rewards. We must ask ourselves *"What do we truly risk losing and what do we stand to gain?"* This approach hobbles our obsession with the risks associated with a decision and spurs us to objectively weigh the risks against the potential rewards.

The second tactic is to imagine the worst-case scenario of a decision. Oftentimes, this scenario, when viewed through an objective lens, isn't nearly as catastrophic as we imagine. Recognizing this fact allows us to quell our baseless fears and move forward.

#7 - Survivorship Bias

We tend to give more credence to people, events, and ideas that succeed and flourish than to those that don't. In many cases, we simply ignore the latter. This is called survivorship bias. It's a mental shortcut that causes us to pay attention to visibly successful subgroups of larger groups and assign excessive authority or importance to them.

For example, suppose you're thinking of opening a restaurant. You've read about successful restauranteurs like Gordon Ramsey, Jamie Oliver, and Tilman Fertitta. Their accomplishments convince you that your restaurant can also thrive. It's possible to overlook the objective data surrounding the business of running a restaurant. These data include the fact that 60% of restaurants fail within one year of opening and 80% fail within five years.

This is an example of survivorship bias. It's a form of tunnel vision. We acknowledge success stories and ignore stories about failure. Consequently, we put too much stock in the former and not enough in the latter. This often leads to overoptimism and overconfidence, both of which impede our ability to make rational decisions. Just because Bill Gates and Mark Zuckerberg dropped out of college and subsequently became successful business owners doesn't mean we can follow in their footsteps and replicate their success.

HOW TO OVERCOME IT: We can counteract survivorship bias in our decision-making in three ways. First, we must scrutinize the validity of our information. How reliable is it? Were we overly selective in choosing sources, giving undue priority to examples of success?

Second, we should assume we're not seeing the entire picture, particularly if we've fallen victim to survivorship bias in the past. We should ask ourselves "what are we missing" and "where are our blind spots?"

Third, we should scrutinize whether any example of success is an outlier. Is the example of success a fair representative of the larger group from which the example is drawn? Or is it a deviation from the norm? A statistical oddity? If so, we should adjust our weighting of its significance accordingly.

#8 - Action Bias

This bias compels us to take action, even when we don't know what to do. We feel that doing something (*anything!*) is better than doing nothing. We prioritize action over inaction, convinced the former will result in a better outcome than the latter.

For example, suppose you're not feeling well, and you're unsure of the reason. Without knowing the root cause of your ailment, there's no way to know how to resolve it. Despite this fact, you may still feel compelled to take an over-the-counter medication. You have the urge to do *something* rather than do nothing.

Another example, one that's often cited to describe the action bias, is the decision of a soccer goalkeeper during a penalty kick. Most goalkeepers will choose to jump either left or right to block the kick. But studies show they have a better chance of successfully blocking penalty kicks by simply remaining still.[1] Statistically, inaction would lead to a better outcome than action.

Yet few soccer goalkeepers follow this approach to block penalty kicks. This is the action bias in action.

When we take action without good reason - i.e. to avoid *inaction* - we risk making bad decisions that lead to undesirable outcomes. We act on impulse rather than choosing a logical course of action after careful analysis of pertinent information.

. . .

How to overcome it: The first step toward controlling the action bias is to recognize that doing nothing is not the same as conceding defeat. Nor does it stem from a lack of courage or commitment. Choosing to do nothing often demonstrates patience and self-control, both of which can be productive.

A second tactic is to ask ourselves *"Am I required to make a decision at this moment?"* Asking this question pushes back against our impulse to act. It's often enough to stave off the compulsion, giving us time to think through the risks and rewards of taking immediate action. It gives us a chance to recognize that *inaction* may be the most productive path forward - at least, at this moment.

#9 - Self-Serving Bias

This bias encourages us to take credit for our successes while attributing circumstances beyond our control for our failures. Social psychologists claim the tendency stems from a need to protect our self-esteem.

For example, suppose you're taking an important exam. If you do well on the exam, you may attribute your success to the fact that you studied for hours. If you do poorly, you might blame your poor performance on the professor's teaching style. Or the temperature in the room during the exam. Or the fact that your neighbors prevented you from getting to sleep the night before.

Or suppose you're making a sales presentation to an important client. If you successfully make the sale, you might credit your insight into the client's needs. If you fail to make the sale, you may blame the situation on the client's bad mood.

The self-serving bias derails the decision-making process because it encourages us to overlook our shortcomings while falsely blaming mistakes on external factors. It creates blindspots. We overestimate our abilities and knowledge while underestimating the risks and hazards stemming from our limitations.

HOW TO OVERCOME IT: We can do two specific things to counteract this bias. First, we must recognize the impulse to cast blame on external factors when we fail. This impulse is instinctive so it may not be immediately obvious to us. We must learn to be conscious of this behavior. Simple awareness gives us a chance to self-correct when this bias arises.

Second, we must acknowledge that we make mistakes. We're imperfect so mistakes are inevitable. Admitting this to ourselves encourages us to take responsibility for our failures. It emboldens us to be accountable for our choices and actions. While this accountability may seem scary, it ultimately gives us greater agency in our decision-making.

#10 - Authority Bias

This bias compels us to favor the opinions of authority figures over the opinions of non-authority figures. It makes us predisposed to give excessive weight to the former. This compulsion is common and occurs in every aspect of our lives. This is the case because most of us are naturally obliged to follow authority - to cede to leaders. It's instinctual.

Perhaps the greatest example of this tendency is the famous Milgram experiment. Conducted by Stanley Milgram at Yale University, participants were divided into two groups: "teachers" and "learners." Teachers were instructed by an "experimenter" (the authority) to ask questions of the learners.

The learners were, unknown to the teachers, actors. They were strapped to chairs and connected to electrodes. When learners responded to questions with incorrect answers, teachers were instructed to deliver what they were told was a painful shock. Teachers were also told to increase the intensity of the shock with each incorrect answer.

Milgram wanted to know how far the teachers would go to follow orders. He found most would continue to deliver the ostensibly painful shocks, even while watching the learners pretend to writhe in agony. The reason? Simply because they were instructed to do so by an authority figure (the "experimenter"). When a few teachers balked, they were prodded to continue, which they ultimately did.

The authority bias can obviously have a deleterious effect on our decisions. It can cause us to overlook or disregard important variables. It can make us inclined to give undue credence to select information just because the information originates from a perceived authority.

How to overcome it: While this bias is one of the most common, it's also one of the easiest to counteract. There are two tactics we can use toward that end. First, we should instinctively ask ourselves whether the authority figure is truly an expert in the field about which he or she opines. For example, when celebrities opine about governmental policies, how much weight should we give their opinions?

Second, we should question whether the authority figure is incentivized to offer a particular opinion. For example, a doctor who advocates use of a particular medication may be awarded for doing so by the pharmaceutical company that created it. A car salesperson's compensation is tied to the price of the vehicles displayed on the lot.

The Road Forward

We've covered a lot of material in this chapter. I've included it because I consider cognitive biases to represent the largest obstacle to our ability to make good decisions. These biases negatively affect every aspect of our lives. They impair our decisions at home, in the workplace, and at school. They mislead us when we make decisions that impact our careers, relationships, and ultimately our quality of life.

While these biases will not be referenced by name in *Part II: 14 Tactics for Making Better Decisions*, it's important to realize that they pose an ever-present stumbling block. The good news is, you now have the tools to outsmart them. You know how to recognize them along with specific tactics to limit their influence.

In the following section, we'll take a quick look at a psychological phenomenon that can limit our capacity to make well-reasoned decisions. You've undoubtedly experienced it. You'll now discover why it happens and how you can counteract it.

---

1. Bar-Eli, M., Azar, O.H., Ritov, I., Keidar-Levin, Y., and Schein, G. (2007). "Action bias among elite soccer goalkeepers: The case of penalty kicks." *Journal of Economic Psychology*. 28(5), 606-621. DOI: 10.1016/j.joep.2006.12.001

THE ROLE OF DECISION FATIGUE

> 66 I am not a product of my circumstances. I am a product of my decisions.
>
> — STEPHEN R. COVEY

All of us suffer from decision fatigue. It impacts us every day of our lives. Alarmingly, it usually happens without our realization. It's as inconspicuous as it is exhaustive, and can be particularly disruptive to our decision-making process. Decision fatigue can cause us to make unhealthy, irrational choices even when we know those choices are contrary to our goals.

Below, I'll explain how decision fatigue occurs and how it affects our ability to make healthy, well-reasoned, and productive decisions. I'll then share several strategies you can start using immediately to make yourself less vulnerable to it.

Decision Fatigue Explained

Think about the last time you came home after a difficult, stressful day at your job. Attending back-to-back meetings, negotiating with exasperating clients and coworkers, and putting out an endless series of fires left you feeling exhausted, both physically and emotionally. You craved peace and relaxation. You spent the entire day making decisions, both substantive and trivial, and now, at the end of the day, feel entirely spent.

Let's suppose you'd normally don your workout clothes, grab your running shoes, and go for a jog. Jogging helps you to clear your head and gives you a chance to exercise. But today is different. You feel completely worn out. So instead you choose to lay on your couch with an armful of junk food and watch Netflix.

You've succumbed to decision fatigue.

Decision fatigue refers to our diminishing ability to make good choices due to the volume of decisions we've made up to that point in time. This ability behaves like a vehicle's fuel tank. Our tank is full when we wake up in the morning. But each decision we make consumes fuel. The more decisions we make, the more fuel we consume. At the end of the day, after making hundreds of decisions, our tank is empty. Our decision-making ability has become severely impaired.

Many people assume their poor choices are due to a lack of willpower. In reality, they possess willpower. But long decision-making sessions steadily chip away at it.

Again, this phenomenon happens to everyone. No one is immune to it. For example, a study published in 2011 showed that judges' legal decisions were influenced by the number of decisions they made and their resulting tiredness.[1] The percentage of their rulings favoring prisoners declined markedly as the day progressed without breaks.

These judges had succumbed to decision fatigue (to the prisoners' misfortune).

How Decision Fatigue Adversely Affects Your Life

It's crucial that we recognize the far-reaching effects of decision fatigue. It negatively influences our choices in every area of our lives. It governs our resolve and commitment at our jobs. It sways how we manage our money. It impels our behaviors at home, at school, and when we're with our friends and loved ones.

For example, suppose you're at your workplace focused on a large project for which you're responsible. You've spent the day making countless decisions and now feel drained. In this state, you're more likely to cut corners on the quality of your work.

Or suppose you're at the grocery store in the evening to pick up needed items. Normally, you'd disregard the junk food found at the checkout counter. But because you've had an exhausting day of intensive decision-making, your ability to make wise choices is compromised. So when you notice candy, chips, and cookies that are on sale, you uncharacteristically purchase them.

Or suppose you're visiting a restaurant with friends. You ordinarily enjoy a glass of wine with your meal. Knowing your low tolerance for alcohol, you typically refrain from consuming more than a single glass. But due to an especially-taxing day during which you were forced to make innumerable decisions, your ability to self-regulate is weakened. Consequently, one glass of wine turns into three.

Decision fatigue affects us in ways that are often unnoticeable to us. Its inconspicuous nature makes us especially vulnerable to stress and low performance, impulsiveness, and a diminished ability to monitor our emotions, thoughts, and actions. It makes us more susceptible to the cognitive biases we discussed in the previous chapter. Decision fatigue can even lead to decision *avoidance*, where we freeze up and become reluctant to make decisions altogether

So let's explore some simple strategies we can use, starting today, to combat decision fatigue.

7 Tactics for Overcoming Decision Fatigue

IT ISN'T feasible to continually avoid making decisions. That would prevent us from accomplishing anything. So we must rely on other measures to resist decision fatigue and the feelings of burnout and exhaustion that accompany it.

1. Create routines that make decisions for you

Recall the "fuel tank" analogy from earlier. Even small decisions consume fuel. So establish routines that make these small choices for you.

For example, wake up at the same time each morning. Eat the same food for breakfast. Stick to the same workout regimen each day. And rather than choosing when to do your laundry during the week, commit to doing it each Saturday morning.

There are undoubtedly numerous decisions you can circumvent by creating these small routines.

2. Take advantage of automation

The fewer decisions you're forced to make, the better you'll be able to withstand decision fatigue. There are many tools that can automate select decisions.

For example, set up auto payment for bills that must be paid each month (electric bill, car payments, etc.). Create an auto investment program that transfers money from your checking account into a mutual fund each month. If you receive a lot of email that doesn't require an immediate response (or any response at all), create filters in your email program to automatically place them into folders for later perusal.

3. Address important decisions first

Some decisions have greater priority than others. Tackle those before you address lower-priority decisions.

For example, suppose you need to choose a supplier from which to buy materials for your business. Your choice will have far-reaching impacts. It will affect the quality of your products and govern their availability. It may dictate the extent to which you can expand your product line down the road. Rather than postponing this important decision until later in the day, tackle it as early as possible.

Remember the "fuel tank" analogy? There's always more fuel in the tank in the morning than in the afternoon or evening.

4. Simplify low-impact decisions

Many decisions are complicated because we unnecessarily make them so. The more complicated the decision, the more decision-making "fuel" it will consume. With that in mind, if a choice between multiple options will have minimal impact on your goals, simplify it.

For example, rather than choosing what to wear each day, build a wardrobe comprised of similar-looking attire. That'll make your choices simpler. If you regularly volunteer to bring food to friendly get-togethers, have a small list of dishes you normally prepare for such occasions. Don't agonize over the decision. If you need to purchase an ethernet cable for your home, immediately choose one with an acceptable length and move on rather than dallying over the legion of options.

5. Eat something before making important decisions

Sounds simple, right? Perhaps even too simple. But that means this tactic is commonly overlooked.

Eating replenishes your stores of glucose. Replenishing these stores improves your ability to make good decisions.[2] Have you ever felt hungry and found it difficult to focus? Ever skipped lunch and become irritable and impatient? All of us have experienced this. Lack of glucose impairs self-regulation and increases impulsiveness. Neither result in good decisions.

So, whenever you need to make an important decision, eat something healthy. Replenish the "fuel" in your tank.

6. Learn how to say no

Many decisions are foisted upon us by others. Coworkers ask us for unreasonable favors (e.g. they implore us to handle time-intensive tasks for which they're responsible). Acquaintances request our help when they have other options (e.g. they want us to help them move when they can easily hire professional movers). Friends and family may fail to recognize our boundaries (e.g. they regularly drop by without calling).

Get comfortable with saying "no." You can do so with grace and respect, and eliminate decisions in the process.

It's difficult at first. But it gets easier with experience. The upside is, if you are consistent in saying no to particular types of requests, you'll force others to modify their expectations of you. And that will discourage them from forcing such decisions on you in the future.

7. Minimize distractions

Most of the distractions that surround us each day add little value to our lives. They may be interesting to us. They might even satisfy our inner voyeurs. But if they suddenly ceased to exist, our lives wouldn't be negatively impacted in any serious way.

Meanwhile, distractions obstruct our ability to make good decisions. They divert our attention and erode our focus. They cause us to examine irrelevant information, wasting valuable time and attentional resources. They obfuscate our options, constraining our perspective and limiting our insight.

For these reasons, it's important to ignore inconsequential distractions whenever you need to make major decisions. For example, shun social media. Steer clear of trivial conversations between coworkers. Disregard non-urgent phone calls and texts from friends. The fewer distractions that you allow to sidetrack your attention, the easier you'll find it to make decisions. This alone will help keep decision fatigue at bay.

Coming up Next...

All of the material we've covered in *Part I: Understanding Our Decision-Making Process* has laid the groundwork for what we're going to cover in *Part II: 14 Tactics for Making Better Decisions*. In the next section, we'll go through a number of systems you can use to improve your decision-making. These are the tools that will help you to produce better outcomes from your choices in every imaginable area of your life.

---

1. Danziger, Shai, Levav, Jonathan, and Avnaim-Pesso, Liora (2011). "Extraneous factors in judicial decisions." *Proceedings of the National Academy of Sciences.* 108 (17) 6889-6892. DOI: 10.1073/pnas.1018033108 https://www.pnas.org/content/108/17/6889

2. Orquin, Jacob L. and Kurzban, Robert (2016). "A meta-analysis of blood glucose effects on human decision making." *Psychological Bulletin.* PMID: 26653865. DOI: 10.1037/bul0000035 https://pubmed.ncbi.nlm.nih.gov/26653865/

PART II

14 TACTICS FOR MAKING BETTER DECISIONS

We'll rarely possess all of the information we need to make a decision with absolute confidence regarding the outcome. There will always exist uncertainty. The information we need will sometimes be difficult to obtain, and the time and effort required to obtain it may be a poor investment given its anticipated impact. Other times, we'll be hampered by blind spots, prejudices, and biases that threaten to derail our decision-making process. So it's safe to assume we'll always operate at some level of unawareness.

This section of *How to Make Better Decisions* will provide you with tools you can use to minimize the effect of unknown variables and counterproductive factors. Most of these tactics are simple (the most useful ones usually are). A few are slightly complex. Together, they'll help you to analyze situations methodically and make reasoned choices given the information available to you.

These tools provide a second benefit: they'll encourage you to take action. When faced with uncertainty, many of us are tempted to hold off making decisions. We feel insufficiently equipped to choose wisely between conflicting options. Consequently, we become hampered by *indecision*. The tactics in *Part II* will spur you to take sensible, strategic action, even in the face of uncertainty.

One last note before we proceed...

As mentioned earlier, each chapter in this section ends with an exercise. You may be tempted to gloss over them, promising yourself that you'll do them at some later date. I strongly encourage you to do the exercises as you read the chapters. You'll benefit from the continuity of the content, learning how each tactic works and then putting it into practice.

These exercises serve two purposes. First, they'll increase your awareness of common decision-making mistakes that lead to regrettable outcomes. The exercises will help you to practice sidestepping them.

Second, they'll demonstrate how *easily* the tactics described in *Part II* can be used to evaluate your options and make well-reasoned, shrewd decisions. Most people make decisions based on intuition and gut instinct, and are then surprised when their results are unfavorable. Doing the exercises will reveal how simply (and deftly) you can avoid similarly poor outcomes.

Fair warning: the exercises require a bit of time and focus. But rest assured, it's a good investment. If you complete the exercises, I promise your investment will pay significant dividends down the road.

With that said, let's roll up our sleeves and get to work…

TACTIC #1: IDENTIFY YOUR DESIRED OUTCOME (AND WHY IT'S IMPORTANT TO YOU)

 Greatness is not a function of circumstance. Greatness, it turns out, is largely a matter of conscious choice, and discipline.

— JIM COLLINS

It's important to know *exactly* what we'd like to achieve before we make consequential decisions. This awareness focuses our attention and drives our efforts. It gives us purpose and motivation. It spurs us to organize and manage our resources so we're making the most of them.

You've no doubt heard the maxim "start with the end in mind." That's precisely how we should approach decision-making.

Knowing our desired outcome also helps to ensure the choices we make align with our personal values. When our choices and values are in alignment, we feel more invested in our circumstances. We also feel more empowered and responsible for the results of our decisions. We experience a greater sense of agency.

When we fail to identify our desired outcome, and in the process disregard our personal values, we become rudderless. We become less able to recognize the gravity of our circumstances and the consequences that accompany conflicting options. Worse, losing sight of our core principles, we lose our motivation to make choices that feel right to us. We lose the measuring stick by which we determine what is truly meaningful to us.

So how can we make certain that we're aware of our desired outcome and make choices that align with our values? We do so by asking ourselves - and candidly answering - the following four questions:

1. "What do I want to achieve?"

Be as specific as possible.

2. "Why do I want to achieve this outcome?"

Our resources are limited. There's never enough money, time, and attention to allocate to everything we want to accomplish. So achieving this particular outcome means postponing or abandoning *other* outcomes. Given this limitation, why is this one important to us?

3. "What will be required of me to achieve this outcome?"

To recognize the importance of a particular outcome, we must know what we'll need to sacrifice to bring it to fruition. We need to know how much money, time, and attention (our three most limited resources) we'll need to invest. Clarifying this matter allows us to quantify the required investment. This in turn helps us to compare the outcome against others, and better judge which should be given the higher priority.

4. "Does this outcome complement my core values?"

Imagine that your decision has produced your desired results. How do you feel? Do the results align with - or detract from - your personal identity?

Our values are entwined in every decision we make. Our choices ultimately reflect who we are at our core. This is the reason bad choices sometimes make us feel terrible. They're often out of alignment with our convictions.

LET's put the above into practice.

Exercise #1

CONSIDER a goal that's important to you. This goal might be related to your health, career, travel, or financial stability. Perhaps you'd like to improve a particular relationship, learn a new skill, or pursue higher education. For the purpose of this exercise, let's suppose you'd like to save $100,000.

First, ask yourself why you want to save this amount of money. Do you wish to do so in order to build an emergency fund? Is it to bolster your retirement? Is it to pay for your child's college tuition?

Next, identify the resources you'll need to dedicate toward realizing this outcome. The primary resource in this example will be money, of course. Accordingly, how much money will you need to set aside each month? Note that this money cannot be allocated for other purposes. Identifying a specific amount will help you to determine the importance of *this* outcome when compared against others that also require funds (travel, pursuit of an advanced degree, purchase of a house, etc.).

Finally, ask yourself whether saving $100,000 for the purpose you intend is consistent with your values. For example, let's say you're doing this to pay for your child's college tuition. Does paying for his or her tuition align with your personal identity? Does it reflect who you are at your core? Imagine that you've successfully saved $100,000 and placed the funds into an account earmarked for your intended purpose. How do you feel?

Time required: 15 minutes

TACTIC #2: REDUCE THE INFLUENCE OF LOSS AVERSION

66 In any moment of decision, the best thing you can do is the right thing, the next best thing is the wrong thing, and the worst thing you can do is nothing.

— THEODORE ROOSEVELT

We discussed loss aversion in *Part I: Understanding Our Decision-Making Process.* We defined the tendency, clarified how it occurs, and examined its adverse effect on our choices. In this section, we'll work to minimize its influence on us.

Loss aversion is based on fear. We dread losing something we value and will go to great lengths to prevent doing so. This "something" may come in the form of money or it might be a relationship, article of clothing, or the freedom that comes with having options. Marketers regularly use loss aversion to motivate consumers to buy things regardless of need (e.g. *"Only 8 hours remaining before prices increase!"*).

Loss aversion sometimes has practical value. An example is auto insurance. We purchase insurance to insulate ourselves from the financial repercussions associated with getting into traffic accidents or suffering damage to our vehicles. Another example is diversifying our investments. Rather than allowing a single stock to make up our entire portfolio, we invest in numerous stocks or mutual funds. This is an attempt to minimize the risk of financial loss.

The problem is, when loss aversion is left unchecked, it can wreak havoc with our ability to make reasoned decisions. Rather than helping us to *mitigate* risk, it induces us to consider *all* risk as undesirable. This mindset leads to indecision and an unwillingness to accept risk as a normal tradeoff in decision-making.

So how do we counteract loss aversion while making decisions? Fortunately, there are a number of simple measures we can take to limit its effect on us. Following are four things we can do immediately.

1. Reframe Decisions from a Binary "Gain/Loss" Model

When we're overly concerned about a potential loss, we tend to perceive our situation in terms of a "gain/loss" paradigm. We win or we lose. Those are the only two outcomes in our minds. This is an unrealistic model because it ignores the nuances, or gradations, of the potential gain and loss.

For example, suppose we're thinking about investing $10,000 into a mutual fund. Loss aversion causes us to worry about losing our $10,000 if the stock market suffers a severe blow. It ignores the fact that losses are rarely, if ever, absolute. In a bear market, we may indeed lose money. But the loss is highly unlikely to be complete. Rather, it's likely to be a small percentage of our investment (e.g. 10% or $1,000).

One way to counter the influence of loss aversion on our decision-making is to reframe our choices. Rather than think in terms of whether we stand to gain or lose, we should ponder *how much* we stand to gain and *how much* we risk losing. We change our perspective to highlight the nuances of our situation. For example, *how much* might our $10,000 investment grow over the coming years? *How much* of our investment might we truly lose?

Reframing decisions in this manner short circuits loss aversion and defuses the fear that accompanies it.

2. Imagine the Worst-Case Scenario

Remember, loss aversion is based on fear. The problem is, this fear is almost always exaggerated. It causes us to feel vulnerable in a way that is out of alignment with reality.

To illustrate, let's return to our investment example. We fear losing all of our money in the event a bear market occurs. But such a scenario has never happened in the history of the stock market. During the Great Depression in the U.S., the Dow Jones Industrial Average (DJIA) lost 89% of its value. But various measures have since been put into effect to prevent such a thing from happening again. Moreover, analysis shows that had we invested at the absolute *height* of the market in 1929 (i.e. we had the worst timing imaginable), we would have fully recovered by late 1936.

This demonstrates an important lesson. We can overcome loss aversion by considering the worst-case scenario associated with a particular decision. What is the worst that can possibly happen if everything goes wrong? Oftentimes, the worst-case scenario isn't nearly as catastrophic as we initially imagine.

Once we've entertained this extreme predicament, we should ask ourselves two follow-up questions:

1. Can we handle the adversity that accompanies it?
2. Will we eventually recover?

In nearly every case, if we're being honest with ourselves, the answer to both questions will be yes.

3. Filter Unreasonably Pessimistic News and Opinions

Pessimism, which often stems from fear, feeds loss aversion. Whether it comes from "current event" news sources, social media, or your friends, family members, or coworkers, it emphasizes the potential for loss. It encourages catastrophic thinking and reinforces the notion that disaster looms around every corner. Will we lose our jobs? Will we go bankrupt? Will our businesses fail?

This pessimism handicaps our ability to make reasoned, informed decisions. It causes us to give undue credence to our fears concerning potential loss.

A simple way to negate this pessimism is to filter the sources that foster and promote it. If the "current event" news media sites we favor offer nothing but tragedy, drama, and fear, we should disregard them. If social media causes us to become angry and anxious, we should avoid it. If our friends, family members, and coworkers are a constant source of pessimism, we should reject their counsel and disregard their opinions.

Filtering sources of pessimism allows us to avoid unsubstantiated negativity and make rational, logical decisions unencumbered by an intemperate fear of loss.

4. Use a Decision-Making Quadrant

A decision-making quadrant is a simple tool we can use to keep our emotions in check while we analyze our options. Here's how it works:

Draw a vertical line down the middle of a blank piece of paper. Next, draw a horizontal line across the middle. You're left with four quadrants.

- In the top-left quadrant, write "What positives occur if I choose option #1?"
- In the top-right quadrant, write "What positives occur if I *don't* choose option #1?"
- In the bottom-left quadrant, write "What negatives occur if I choose option #1?"
- In the bottom-right quadrant, write "What negatives occur if I *don't* choose option #1?"

This tool, when used properly, will reveal the consequences, both good and bad, associated with each decision. Its analytical nature reduces our susceptibility to the unwarranted fear that accompanies loss aversion.

LET's put the above into practice.

Exercise #2

SUPPOSE you're thinking about leaving your current job for another position. First, determine whether you have an unrealistic "gain/loss" mindset about this decision. If you do, reframe the decision to highlight the subtle rewards and risks associated with it. For example, will you be happier in your new position? Will you enjoy more autonomy? Will you forego career-boosting opportunities by leaving your current job? Will you need to buy a new wardrobe? Will you have to endure a longer commute? Will you become bored at the new position?

Explore these and other nuances.

Second, consider the worst-case scenario. What is the worst possible outcome of leaving your current position for the new job? Perhaps the new position will disappear, effectively leaving you without a job or income. With this predicament in mind, ask yourself whether you can survive. If you have savings, the answer is almost certainly yes. Next, ask yourself whether you can recover. Again, the answer is probably yes. Chances are high that you'll find another position.

Third, identify sources of steady pessimism. Consider news media sites, Facebook and Twitter, and the people who surround you. Start filtering these sources of negativity. If "current event" news focuses on layoffs, and the information isn't applicable to you, avoid it. If Facebook and Twitter are filled with stories about job-related drama, stop visiting them. If friends, family members, or coworkers continuously warn you against leaving your current position, appraise the soundness of their opinions and advice, and disregard both if they're overly fearful.

Finally, create a decision-making quadrant. Follow the steps outlined in #4 above. Blank sheet of paper. Four quadrants. Use it to examine every possible consequence, good and bad, associated with leaving your current job for the new position.

If you go through these four steps, you'll eliminate the fear that accompanies loss aversion. You'll then be able to confidently make a rational decision based on pertinent factors and information.

Time required: 30 minutes

TACTIC #3: DISTINGUISH BETWEEN IMPORTANT AND UNIMPORTANT DECISIONS

 What is important is seldom urgent and what is urgent is seldom important.

— DWIGHT D. EISENHOWER

One of the stumbling blocks to making good decisions is our tendency to confuse those that are urgent with those that are important. This confusion typically manifests as an assumption that *every-thing* is important and warrants our immediate attention. The assumption is nearly always incorrect. And it causes us to feel stressed and exhausted as we struggle to manage one perceived crisis after another.

The quote that leads this section is insightful. Eisenhower understood that the ability to distinguish truly important decisions from the merely urgent ones was a key to success. And he developed a system to help him do so.

Before we discuss this system, now called the Eisenhower Matrix, let's define two basic terms:

Urgent decisions - these demand your immediate attention. They don't necessarily *warrant* your immediate attention. They just demand it. You can often put them on the back burner and sometimes disregard them altogether. When we attend to urgent decisions, we're forced to do so reactively. An example is the choice to respond right away to persistent emails from a coworker. The emails may be urgent. But whether they're *important* is still unknown.

Important decisions - these align with our goals and personal values. They help us to make progress toward whatever we're trying to accomplish. When we attend to them, we're usually able to do so rationally and without panic. We're rarely forced to react to important decisions. We have time to think them through. An example is the decision to exercise. We can create an exercise routine in advance and schedule time for it each day.

Some urgent decisions are truly important. And some important decisions are truly urgent. The Eisenhower Matrix helps us to identify and prioritize *all* decisions and thereby ultimately determine where we should devote our limited attentional resources.

This system makes use of a simple 2 x 2 matrix. The four individual quadrants represent the four types of decisions. Below are the four types starting from the top-left quadrant and following a clockwise pattern...

- urgent & important
- not urgent but important
- neither urgent nor important
- urgent but unimportant

This matrix forces us to consider each decision in terms of its importance and urgency. By doing so, it encourages us to devote our attentional resources to the decisions that are likely to have the greatest impact on our lives. It simultaneously allows us to see which decisions are *least* likely to impact us and can thus be delayed or disregarded.

This system frees up our time. Consequently, it allows us to operate from a state of calm and reason rather than stress and anxiety. This naturally leads to better analysis of our options and ultimately improved decisions and more favorable outcomes.

Let's put the above into practice.

Exercise #3

CREATE a list of all the decisions that currently clamor for your attention. Include both trivial and consequential decisions. List those that require little time and effort as well as those that require far more in both departments. Note the ones that call for significant funds as well as those that require no funds at all.

Next, create an Eisenhower Matrix. I recommend using a blank sheet of paper rather than your computer.

Step 1: Divide the sheet of paper into a 2 x 2 matrix.

Step 2: Label each of the four sections thusly:

- Urgent & important
- Not urgent but important
- Neither urgent nor important
- Urgent but unimportant

Step 3: Place each decision currently on your list in the appropriate quadrant.

For example, suppose you want to start exercising and need to decide when to schedule workouts throughout the week. This isn't an urgent decision. But it *is* an important one as it regards your long-term health. As such, you would place it in the top-right quadrant ("Not urgent but important").

Let's suppose a tax deadline is looming and you need to

decide when to make an appointment to see your accountant. Because of the looming deadline, this decision is both urgent and important. So you'd place it in the top-left quadrant.

Let's say you've received several texts from your friend. He or she wants to shoot the breeze. The volume of texts may imply urgency, but their nature is unimportant. The decision to respond is unimportant and can accordingly be placed in the bottom-left quadrant.

Finally, let's suppose there's a stack of junk mail on your desk. Junk mail is neither urgent nor important. You'll suffer no consequence if you ignore it indefinitely. Therefore, the decision to read it or discard it should be placed in the bottom-right quadrant.

Step 4: Assign time blocks to address each decision you've placed in all quadrants except the bottom-right one.

Step 5: Schedule the decisions found in the top-left quadrant ("Urgent & important") during times when your focus and energy are greatest. Schedule those found in the top-right and bottom-left quadrants ("Not urgent but important" and "Urgent but unimportant," respectively) during times when your focus and energy are waning.

Don't schedule time for the decisions in the bottom-right quadrant ("Neither urgent nor important"). You can ignore them, attend to them when you have free time, or delegate them.

The above may seem like a lot of effort to devote to something we typically do intuitively. The problem is, our intuition is unreliable. This is the reason we often feel frazzled and overwhelmed. We routinely fall into the trap of assuming every decision is both important and urgent. The Eisenhower Matrix allows us to avoid that trap. We can thus devote our attentional resources to decisions that'll help us achieve our most important goals.

Time required: 20 minutes

TACTIC #4: MAKE DECISIONS FASTER WITHOUT FEAR

> The risk of a wrong decision is preferable to the terror of indecision.
>
> — MAIMONIDES

F ear causes indecision. It paralyzes us. It stimulates our natural dread of the unknown and discourages us from making decisions due to the attendant risks. It triggers negative thinking and provokes cognitive biases such as loss aversion.

Having said that, fear is an important emotion. It protects us from negative outcomes. It encourages us to be wary of our circumstances and prompts us to take measures to ensure our well-being. For example, when we get into a vehicle, fear of getting into an accident encourages us to put on our seatbelts. When we walk alone during the evening, fear of attack heightens our situational awareness. It spurs us to walk faster and stay in lighted areas.

Fear as an emotion is both beneficial and detrimental. The question is, how do we manage it when we make decisions? How do we prevent fear from getting in the way of rational analysis while simultaneously using it as a protective mechanism? How can we make good decisions *faster* despite our anxiety of the unknown?

The solution is to create a practical framework that helps us to circumvent the unproductive part of our fear. This framework should highlight *genuine* risks and encourage us to rationally assess them. And finally, it should embolden us to make quick decisions with confidence instead of dawdling over baseless concerns.

It sounds like a tough assignment. But it's simpler than it seems.

The 6-Step Framework for Making Fast Decisions

THIS 6-STEP MODEL will prove useful at your job, at home, or in any circumstance where you need to make effective decisions quickly in the face of uncertainty. We'll use our earlier example of "investing $10,000" to demonstrate how it works.

Step 1: Recall your primary goal

We make decisions to accomplish specific aims. When we face a tough choice and having difficulty moving forward, it's useful to remember the reason we're making that choice in the first place.

For example, let's suppose we're setting aside $10,000 to build an emergency fund. That's our objective. If we're having trouble doing this instead of spending the money, we should remember that building this fund is necessary. It's a financial safeguard that'll protect us from life's unanticipated developments. Recalling the fact that this fund could be vital to our future solvency will erode our hesitance.

Step 2: Identify the most impactful variables

We're often tentative in our decision-making because we feel overwhelmed by a flood of information. We become paralyzed with indecision. When this happens, we should assess which pieces of information carry the greatest impact.

Let's say we intend to invest $10,000 into the stock market. But we're hesitant because we've never invested in stocks. We're unfamiliar with the various types of stocks, how to analyze them, and how taxes on capital gains work. We're uninformed about trading techniques, dollar-cost averaging, and the merits of buying and holding. And then there are different investment vehicles to consider: bonds, mutual funds, ETFs, etc. The prospect of investing in crypto-currencies only adds to the confusion.

Most of these variables are less consequential than they seem, particularly because we're new to investing and investing a relatively small amount. Issues such as taxes on capital gains, security analysis, trading techniques, and crypto-currencies are all but immaterial to us at this moment. We should focus on the factors that carry the most weight:

- Should we buy individual stocks or mutual funds?
- Which stocks and mutual funds show long-term promise? (There are plenty of resources online that regularly highlight such stocks and funds.)
- How long do we intend to leave our money in the stock market? Are we investing to pay for a child's college tuition in seven years? Or is the investment part of our retirement fund to be withdrawn 30 years down the road?

By disregarding all but the most relevant factors, we can avoid feeling overwhelmed. This helps us to make quicker decisions with confidence rather than getting mired in unimportant details.

Step 3: Set a deadline

We often hesitate to make decisions because we allow ourselves the *freedom* to hesitate. Setting a deadline limits the time we give ourselves to mull over our choices. It creates a mild sense of urgency, which pushes us to gather and examine information more quickly.

This is beneficial because the more time we take to make decisions, the less confident we become. We begin to question our vetting of our options along with our ability to choose wisely from among them.

Suppose we're procrastinating investing $10,000. Our hesitance stems from our lack of familiarity with investing. We should therefore set a deadline. For example, let's commit to investing our $10,000 in two weeks' time. This deadline adds useful pressure to the decision. It encourages us to quickly seek out and appraise the most pertinent information, and ultimately take action instead of dawdling.

Step 4: Evaluate legitimate risks

Every decision is accompanied by risk. But not all perceived risks are valid. Our minds often imagine improbable scenarios resulting from our presumed errors in judgment. This causes us to hesitate. So whenever we face a tough decision and find ourselves dragging our feet, we should immediately distinguish between real and imagined risks.

For example, we might delay investing $10,000 in the stock market because we fear losing the entire amount. But this isn't a valid risk. The likelihood of a total loss is infinitesimal. Because a total loss is all but inconceivable, it shouldn't cause us concern.

A *legitimate* risk is that our investment might suffer a small loss if the stock market experiences a downturn. We should certainly take this risk into account when deciding how to invest our $10,000. But even this valid risk is limited by the fact that the market has always recovered from downturns. Therefore, we can expect to recoup small losses over time.

In summary, we should first identify genuine risks attached to our choices. Then, we should assess the likelihood that an undesired outcome might occur (and persist). Often, the consequences associated with legitimate risks are less serious than we imagine and easily mitigated.

Step 5: Stress test your personal values

When our choices reflect our core values, we feel confident. We feel like we're doing the right thing. When our choices are *contrary* to our values, we feel ill at ease, as if we're about to make a grave mistake. This latter feeling understandably makes us reluctant to take action. It serves as a natural safeguard against making decisions we'll regret down the road.

If we find ourselves stalling on making a decision, our hesitance might stem from this issue. So we should determine upfront whether our choices match our values or contradict them.

For example, we might hesitate to invest because many companies treat their employees poorly, produce harmful products, or maintain facilities that hurt the environment. Investing in such companies feels wrong to us. If that's the case, we might feel more comfortable, and thus be less likely to hesitate, investing in socially-responsible companies.

Step 6: Accept that uncertainty is a given

We will rarely, if ever, be 100% certain of the outcome that results from a decision. There will always be a risk that our choices lead to unanticipated developments. We attempt to minimize this risk by gathering and evaluating information relevant to our situation, but we won't be able to *eliminate* the risk. That being so, we should accept that uncertainty will always accompany our decisions.

For example, if we invest $10,000 into the stock market, it's not a certainty that our investment will grow at the same pace the market has grown over the last century. The market may suffer a serious downturn. Or a long-term "bull market" might ensue, causing our investment to grow much *faster* than we had anticipated.

We're unable to control every factor that might affect the outcomes of our choices. If we can accept this fact, we can prevent uncertainty from paralyzing us.

.   .   .

LET'S put the above into practice.

∽

Exercise #4

∽

FOR THIS EXERCISE, let's suppose you're considering purchasing a new vehicle. It's a big decision. Naturally, you want to choose wisely. At the same time, you don't want to draw the process out unnecessarily.

Let's use the above framework to speed things up where it makes sense to do so.

First, call to mind your main goal. Let's assume you want to purchase a vehicle that's reliable, affordable, stylish, and fuel-efficient. But your *priority* is reliability. This is your primary goal.

Second, consider the factors that will have the greatest impact on your decision. These might include price, availability, and whether a particular model fits your lifestyle (e.g. a sports car may be unsuitable if you have small children).

Third, set a deadline. Because this is a big decision, you may be tempted to delay making it. To counter this temptation, pick a date on your calendar and commit to choosing a vehicle by that date.

Fourth, identify genuine risks. Will your insurance costs be higher than you expect? Will the new vehicle suffer unanticipated mechanical problems? Will it be too small for your family or too large to fit in your garage? If you identify these legitimate risks upfront, you can take steps to minimize the likelihood they'll negatively impact you.

Fifth, test your choices against your personal values. Perhaps you find a particular automaker's treatment of its employees to be shameful. Or maybe you feel that large vehicles are bad for the environment. Note these affronts to your core values.

Sixth, accept that the result of your decision may differ from your expectation. Remember, you cannot control every factor. For example, you may end up with a "lemon" despite the fact that the automaker has a long history of manufacturing reliable vehicles. Recognize that such outcomes are entirely beyond your influence, and thus should not cause you to hesitate.

Time required: 20 minutes

TACTIC #5: LIMIT YOUR OPTIONS

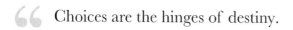 Choices are the hinges of destiny.

— Edwin Markham

We tend to believe having options is an advantage. The more options, the better. It's true to a point. But it's also possible to have so many options in front of us that they impede our decision-making. The seemingly limitless choices make us susceptible to decision fatigue and ultimately lead to indecision.

You've no doubt experienced this effect firsthand. Recall the last time you visited a grocery store to buy an unfamiliar item (e.g. salad dressing). Did the sheer volume of choices seem overwhelming to you? Think back to the last time you picked a novel to read. Did you have difficulty choosing from the millions of titles available? Ever shopped for a piece of furniture and been stunned into indecision by the plethora of options?

Choice is freedom. But choice overload can exhaust and paralyze us. It can also sap our confidence, and even make us feel powerless, with regard to selecting the wisest option.

Fortunately, there's a simple way to avoid this problem: curtail the number of options under our consideration. The fewer options we must consider, the easier it'll be to choose from among them. This tactic will accelerate our decision-making. And as you'll see, it'll do so without forcing us to sacrifice the *quality* of our options. Moreover, this tactic will reward us with greater clarity and peace of mind concerning our selections.

Following are three things you can easily do to reduce the number of options in front of you.

#1 - Reject the overcomplicated options

The greater the complexity of an option, the more suspicious we should be of its merit. While good choices can occasionally be complicated, most are simple. The simplest are usually the ones that deserve our attention. They cause us less stress, encourage us to make faster choices, and often produce the best results.

Let's return to our "invest $10,000" example. Here are

a few of our options when it comes to potential investment vehicles:

- mutual funds
- stocks
- bonds
- derivatives
- options contracts
- commodity futures
- cryptocurrencies (e.g. bitcoin)

Some of the above choices are simple. Some are complex. And a couple are more complex than they seem. For example, investing in bonds *seems* simple until we're forced to consider the huge variety of bond types (government bonds, corporate bonds, high-yield bonds, municipal bonds, etc.). The volume of choices can feel overwhelming.

But suppose we eliminate bonds, derivatives, options, futures, and cryptocurrencies from the list. Now, we only have to choose between investing our money into stocks or mutual funds. It's a much simpler decision. It feels far less intimidating. We can thus decide more quickly and with more confidence. Moreover, if we do our research and choose promising stocks or mutual funds, we can expect positive results.

Getting rid of the complicated choices has cost us nothing. On the contrary, it has saved us time, made our decision easier, and provided us peace of mind.

#2 - Rank options according to their impact on our goal

As we noted in *Tactic #4: Make Decisions Faster Without Fear*, we make decisions to achieve specific goals. The choices we are presented with will have varying levels of impact. Some will greatly affect our goals. Others will have minimal effect. We can drastically reduce our options by ranking them according to the degree and nature of their impact and eliminating those that rank poorly.

For example, let's say we want to invest $10,000 to fund our retirement in the distant future. Thus, we're interested primarily in growth, or capital appreciation. Now, let's consider the following investment vehicles (ranked as described above):

- mutual funds
- stocks
- bonds
- derivatives
- options contracts
- commodity futures
- cryptocurrencies
- foreign exchange market
- annuities
- certificates of deposit
- money market account
- savings account

Some of the above choices do not offer the level of growth we need given our goal. These include savings accounts, money market accounts, CDs, and annuities. Their impact on our goal is minimal, and we can thus eliminate them.

A few choices can greatly impact our goal, but may do so in a negative manner due to their volatility. These include the foreign exchange market, cryptocurrencies, futures, options, and derivatives. These choices can also be disregarded.

We're left with mutual funds, stocks, and bonds. Our decision has been made simpler and easier by ranking and removing the options that pose minimal or an undesirable impact to our main goal (capital appreciation).

#3 - Consider your restrictive preferences

Our choices will usually be limited by certain constraints. These can include our budget, time, and core values. They might involve personal "deal-breakers" that agitate our sensibilities or run contrary to our preferences. We can limit the number of options we face by measuring each according to how well (or poorly) it fares against these constraints.

For example, suppose we've decided to invest $10,000 into mutual funds. There are thousands of mutual funds available, and there's no way to reasonably investigate each one. So let's prune our choices.

First, many mutual funds require an initial investment larger than $10,000. These can be disregarded.

Second, many funds are conservative, investing primarily in low-yield bonds and cash equivalents. If we're interested in capital appreciation, these too can be disregarded.

Third, many funds offer high potential returns, but take massive risks. If we're risk-averse, we should reject these options, as well.

Fourth, some funds welcome small initial investments and take reasonable risks in pursuit of capital appreciation, but come with outrageous expense ratios. We can justifiably eliminate them, too.

Additional restrictions might warrant our consideration based on our preferences. The point is, we can dramatically limit our options in this manner. Doing so will simplify our decision.

LET's put the above into practice.

Exercise #5

FOR THIS EXERCISE, let's suppose you're thinking about making a career change. Given that your decision will probably impact your income, your happiness, and your family, it's important to use caution and carefully investigate your options. That said, there are too many options to fully research. So let's trim the list.

First, focus on the choices that seem overcomplicated. Their complexity may be due to their requiring additional schooling, training, or certification. You might have to endure a long apprenticeship. Or you may need to develop a network of people who can help you lock down a desired position. If you lack the time and/or willingness to clear these hurdles, remove these options from your list.

Second, rank the career choices remaining on your list by the degree and nature of their impact on your goal. Suppose your goal is twofold: high pay and job satisfaction. Your final choice must meet both standards. Some jobs may be emotionally fulfilling, but pay poorly (e.g. being a dog sitter, guitar teacher, or photographer). Others may pay well, but impose high stress (e.g. being an IT manager or defense lawyer). Remove these choices from your list.

Third, consider your personal restrictions. These are the job attributes you want to avoid. They can run the gamut from long hours and high stress to low pay and travel requirements. Many career choices will fare poorly. For example, lawyers often put in long hours. Firefighters usually cope with high stress. Professional cooks often receive low pay. Salespeople frequently travel to visit current and prospective clients. Remove the career choices that fare poorly against your constraints.

The more you can limit your options, the easier you'll find it to focus on the ones most likely to help you achieve your goal.

Time required: 30 minutes

TACTIC #6: PERFORM A GO/NO-GO EVALUATION

> More is lost by indecision than wrong decision. Indecision is the thief of opportunity.

> — MARCUS TULLIUS CICERO

~

Many of us struggle with a predisposition for "going with our gut" when making decisions. We know intuitively that doing so is unwise. Yet the urge is often irrepressible.

There's a reason for this: it's hardcoded into our minds. Our ancestors relied on their gut instincts for survival. It helped them to make quick decisions when information was limited. These days, however, we can quickly and easily obtain more information than is helpful to us. We no longer need to rely on our gut.

The Go/No-Go Evaluation all but eliminates this dependency. This model is typically used by business analysts to determine whether companies should move forward with select projects. For them, it involves feasibility studies, painstaking financial analysis, and collaboration with subject matter experts.

We don't need to go this far. Not even close. With a few smart tweaks, we can create a Go/No-Go Evaluation model that's both easy and effective for our day-to-day decisions. It'll serve the same purpose as it does for business analysts, but stripped of unnecessary complexity.

Let's boil the model down to four simple steps.

The 4-Step Go/No-Go Evaluation Process

MUCH OF OUR decision-making involves whether we should take advantage of considered opportunities. For example, should we take on a promising new client for our fledgling business? Should we move to a new city, state, or province? Should we get an advanced degree, adopt a child, or take a once-in-a-lifetime vacation?

With such decisions, our main impediment is resources. Do we possess the time, attention, and financial means to pursue a given opportunity? The following 4-step Go/No-Go model will prevent us from making a poor decision due to overoptimism.

Step 1: Gather pertinent information

As always, we must possess relevant information to make a rational, productive decision. To that end, we should ask ourselves the following questions:

- What information do I need?
- Where do I find useful sources?
- How do I acquire the information?

Next, we spend time collecting this information. We might rely on online resources, other people (or departments at our job), or even the results of similar decisions we've made in the past.

For example, let's again suppose we're deciding how to invest $10,000. If we're considering investing in stocks, we might review analysts' reports. If we're considering mutual funds, we could use Morningstar reports to compare the best ones given our goals. We can seek advice from a financial advisor. Or we might talk to a family member who has extensive investment experience.

Step 2: Identify and review factors that impact the decision

Brainstorm factors that will influence our decision. These are variables that make the opportunity we're considering seem either more or less appealing or feasible to us.

For example, here are a few deciding factors that will impact how we choose to invest $10,000:

- our risk tolerance
- competing financial demands (emergency fund, home repairs, etc.)
- competing opportunities (family vacation, purchasing a new car, etc.)
- Our time horizon (how soon do we need the money?)

These factors will make some options more attractive or viable and others less so. In fact, they'll help us to confidently remove some of the options from our list as they fail to meet our standards and constraints. (This step is a convenient complement to *Tactic #5: Limit Your Options*.)

Step 3: Assess the risks and potential rewards associated with each option

Before we commit to any option, we must examine what we stand to lose and what we stand to gain by selecting it. We must weigh the associated benefits against the hazards. Step 3 urges us to carefully explore this matter.

Assign a value from 1 to 5 for each risk and each reward as it relates to each option. The higher the assigned value, the greater the option's presumed risk or reward. At the end of this step, we'll tally the respective scores for the options under consideration. Some of the scores will highlight options that should be removed from our list.

For example, let's suppose we're considering investing $10,000 into one of the following four investment vehicles:

1. index funds
2. growth Stocks
3. bonds
4. cryptocurrencies (e.g. bitcoin)

We'll assume we have a high risk tolerance, short investment time horizon, and no higher-priority competing needs nor opportunities for the money. As such, following is how we might score each of the four options with regard to their respective risk/reward profiles.

Index funds

- Risk: 3
- Reward: 4

Growth stocks

- Risk: 3
- Reward: 4

Municipal bonds

- Risk: 1

- Reward: 2

Cryptocurrencies

- Risk: 5
- Reward: 5

Let's now calculate a "net reward" score for each of the above options. To do this, we'll subtract the risk score from the reward score as follows:

- index funds: 3 minus 2 = net reward of 1
- growth stocks: 4 minus 3 = net reward of 1
- municipal bonds: 2 minus 1 = net reward of 1
- cryptocurrencies: 5 minus 5 = net reward of 0

This net reward score allows us to quickly compare the options and eliminate those that are unappealing to us. In the above example, we can confidently remove cryptocurrencies from our list.

Note that our assignment of values for each risk and reward should correspond to the factors we identified in Step 2. For example, our high risk tolerance and short investment time horizon might make municipal bonds less appealing than index funds. Depending on our needs (e.g. capital appreciation), this alone may be enough to remove municipal bonds from our list.

Step 4: Assign "Go" or "No Go" to each factor

Frame each of the factors we identified in Step 2 as a question that can be answered with either a "yes" or "no." This will allow us to decide on the spot whether we should proceed or abandon the option under consideration.

If a factor measures up (i.e. we answer "yes" to its corresponding question), we assign a "Go." We move forward. On the other hand, if the factor fails to make the grade, we assign a "No Go." We thus forego the option.

For example, let's suppose we're thinking about investing our $10,000 into a "small-cap" mutual fund. Such funds invest primarily in smaller companies. These companies offer more growth potential than their larger counterparts, but carry more risk. Let's do a quick "Go/No-Go" analysis using the factors we listed in Step 2. As in the example in Step 3, we'll assume we have a high risk tolerance, short investment time horizon, and no higher-priority competing needs nor opportunities for the $10,000.

Question #1: Can our risk tolerance accommodate the large swings in portfolio value that small-cap mutual funds often experience? Yes. This factor receives a "Go." We can proceed.

Question #2: Can we prioritize investing our money ahead of other financial demands? Yes. (We assumed that no such demands exist.). This factor receives a "Go." We can proceed.

Question #3: Can we prioritize investing our money ahead of other opportunities for which the money might be used? Yes. (We assumed that no such opportunities exist.). This factor receives a "Go." We can proceed.

Question #4: Can we confidently invest in small-cap funds knowing that we must retrieve our money in twelve months? NO. Our short investment time horizon precludes high-risk investments. While we have a high risk tolerance, it is made less relevant by the fact that we need to withdraw our money in one year's time. Therefore, this factor receives a "No Go," and we immediately abandon small-cap funds as an investment option.

We'll go through this process for each option that remains on our list (index funds, growth stocks, municipal bonds, etc.).

LET's put the above into practice.

Exercise #6

THINK of a decision you're currently facing. Maybe you're considering buying a house. Perhaps you're thinking of making a career change. Or maybe you're facing a smaller decision where the impact of your choice is less intimidating.

For example, let's suppose you're thinking of quitting sugar. The first step toward completing a Go/No-Go Evaluation is to identify the information that'll help you to decide how to proceed. We'll then need to figure out how to obtain it.

For this example, you'll want information regarding how quitting sugar will affect your mood, focus, and energy levels. You'll want to know the long-term effects on your physique and health. Sources of this information include doctors, nutritionists and dietitians, and fitness trainers. You can also find much of it online for free. And of course, you can purchase books that address the subject.

Next, list the factors that will influence your decision regarding whether or not to quit sugar and how to go about doing so. Following are a few examples:

- your ability and willingness to resist cravings
- your tolerance for sugar deprivation
- your ability to endure potential short-term side effects
- your willingness to forego your favorite foods

- your ability to endure others' reactions to the decision

Next, we'll explore the risks and rewards associated with your options. We'll also assign values to them. These values, from 1 to 5, should convey your priorities as well as their degree of impact on you.

Your options in this example are limited to the following:

- Give up sugar completely
- Reduce your sugar consumption
- Maintain the status quo

We'll go through the first option to demonstrate this step. I encourage you to complete this process for the remaining two options. Note: the values I've assigned to each risk and reward below are merely for the example. It's possible you would assign different values based on your preferences and circumstances.

Risks of giving up sugar completely:

- worsened mood (3)
- changes in sleep patterns (4)
- lightheadedness (2)
- fatigue (1)
- anxiety (3)

Total score: 13

The values assigned above indicate that we dread changes in our sleep patterns while fatigue is hardly a concern for us.

Now, the potential rewards of quitting sugar:

- weight loss (4)
- lower risk of select diseases (2)
- better focus (3)
- improved oral health (2)
- improved skin (2)
- better sleep (4)

Total score: 17

Let's calculate our net reward score for this option. 17 minus 13 = 4. Go through this process for the remaining two options. Once you've tallied a net reward score for each of them, you can compare them against each other and decide the most suitable path forward.

The final step is to determine whether each option is feasible. We'll examine each of the factors we identified in Step 2 and frame them as questions that can be answered with a "yes" or "no." Factors that are answered with a "yes" indicate the option is workable. If any factor is answered with a "no," we immediately stop the examination and remove the corresponding option from our list.

Following are the factors, reframed as questions, for our "quitting sugar" example. I've made an assumption for question #4 to demonstrate what happens when we answer "no."

Question #1: Will I be able to resist the cravings for sugary foods? Yes. This factor receives a "Go." We can proceed.

Question #2: Will I be able to tolerate sugar deprivation? Yes. This factor receives a "Go." We can proceed.

Question #3: Will I be able to endure the potential short-term side effects? Yes. This factor receives a "Go." We can proceed.

Question #4: Am I willing to forego my favorite foods? NO.

We can stop the evaluation here. We don't need to answer question #5 (weathering others' reactions to our decision to quit sugar). Our unwillingness to forego our favorite foods makes this option (quitting sugar entirely) impractical. We can confidently remove it from our list and start evaluating the next option (reducing our sugar consumption).

Question #5: n/a

Time required: 30 minutes

Admittedly, the Go/No-Go Evaluation is a complicated decision-making model. But it's highly useful, particularly when we're faced with decisions that carry big risks and big potential rewards.

TACTIC #7: CREATE A WEIGHTED PROS-AND-CONS LIST (THE CORRECT WAY TO DO IT AND 3 PITFALLS TO AVOID)

> 66 There is no decision that we can make that doesn't come with some sort of balance or sacrifice.
>
> — SIMON SINEK

You've no doubt created pros-and-cons lists before. If not formally, by listing items on a piece of paper, then at least doing so in your head. Creating such lists seems like a simple task. But to make a pros-and-cons list truly meaningful, useful, and actionable, we must take a more methodical approach. And with a bit of creativity, we can produce a list that all but tells us the best course of action.

Why Pros-and-Cons Lists Are Valuable Aids in Decision-Making

This tool is particularly useful when we're faced with two simple options: to move forward on a given decision or to abandon it. There are no other viable choices.

In such circumstances, a pros-and-cons list provides us a bird's-eye view of the situation. If constructed properly, it improves our understanding of the relevant issues and gives us a simple, fast way to evaluate one path against the other.

Additionally, the exacting thoroughness required to create an effective pros-and-cons list encourages emotional distance from the problem at hand. The rigor of the process invokes dispassion. That's advantageous as powerful emotions can cause us to make imprudent decisions that lead to poor outcomes.

How to Create an Effective Pros-and-Cons List

THE PROCESS INVOLVES five simple steps. You'll be familiar with most of them, although the final two steps may surprise you. Both of these final steps are critical pieces of the process and can transform your pros-and-cons list from a tool that's moderately helpful into one that literally highlights the optimal choice.

Step #1: Format your list

I recommend doing this on a blank sheet of 8 1/2" x 11" paper, especially if you're a tactile, visual person like myself. The tangibility of your pros-and-cons list will keep you focused and less susceptible to distractions. Having said that, if you're working remotely, need remote access to your lists, or simply prefer using digital tools, do so.

Create four columns. Make the first and third columns wider than the second and fourth columns. Label the first and third columns "Pros" and "Cons," respectively. Label the second and fourth columns "Score."

Step #2: Brainstorm all relevant pros associated with the decision

Many of the advantages will be less than obvious. So while you may be tempted to rush through this step, it's worth taking your time.

Ask yourself focused questions that can help reveal advantages that may otherwise escape your notice. Following are a few such questions:

- What do I stand to gain if I take this course of action?
- How might it contribute to what I hope to accomplish?
- How might it positively impact my situation?

- What are the side benefits associated with this decision?
- What opportunities might open up for me?
- How might I be positioned down the road if I move forward?

Be thorough. No advantage or benefit is too small to be included on the list.

Step #3: Brainstorm all relevant cons associated with the decision

Follow the same pattern as you did in Step 2. In the same way some of the advantages of moving forward may be hidden, so too might some of the *disadvantages*. So again, take your time in populating this section of your pros-and-cons list.

As before, asking pointed questions will help us to bring to light disadvantages that may otherwise go unnoticed. Following are a few examples:

- What am I risking by taking this course of action?
- What must I sacrifice (i.e. what are the opportunity costs)?
- In what ways is moving forward contrary to my goals?
- What negative exposure might I suffer if I take this course of action?

- Will moving forward compromise my position?
- Will it hamper my efforts toward secondary goals down the road?

Similar to Step 2, no disadvantage is too small to be included on your list. The more thorough you are during Steps 2 and 3, the more complete the picture. This will improve your ability to make the correct choice.

Step #4: Score each pro and con

Not all pros and cons will be equally important to you. So we must assign a weighted score to each of them. This score will reflect their respective impacts, and by extension how much influence they should have on your decision.

I recommend using a scoring system of 1 to 5. A score of 1 implies minimal impact while a score of 5 implies maximum impact.

Let's recall our "invest $10,000" example to demonstrate how scoring works. The lists of pros and cons we'll construct below won't be exhaustive, but they'll suffice for illustrative purposes.

Pros of investing $10,000 (and their respective scores between 1 and 5):

- You'll save money for the future (5)
- You'll stay ahead of inflation (2)
- Your portfolio will grow with the economy (3)

- You'll experience peace of mind that you have funds at your disposal (2)
- You'll qualify for an employer-matching program (4)

Cons of investing $10,000 (and their respective scores between 1 and 5):

- Your money will be at risk (4)
- You won't be able to use the money for other purposes (2)
- Your investment may complicate your tax picture (2)
- You'll pay fees, sales charges, and other expenses (3)
- Your money will be less liquid than in a bank account (3)

Now that we've scored each pro and con, we can complete the final and most illuminating step.

Step #5: Tally the scores

Assuming we've properly scored each pro and con in Step 4, the final scores will reveal whether moving forward is a wise decision. Following are the respective tallies from the two lists we constructed above.

Pros of investing $10,000: 16

Cons of investing $10,000: 14

Comparing the two final scores indicates that the pros outweigh the cons. Thus, moving forward with the decision to invest $10,000 is a good one.

This model allows us to examine decisions without emotion and make objective choices. By quantifying the respective impacts of each advantage and disadvantage, we allow the model to reveal to us the optimal path.

Having said that, it's worth noting that the soundness of this model's output is only as good as our inputs. We must score the individual pros and cons accurately if we want the final tallies to be actionable.

3 Pitfalls to Avoid When Creating a Pros-and-Cons List

CREATING pros-and-cons lists is a deceptively simple task. As noted earlier, most of us have created them at some point in our lives. So the process is familiar. The problem is, this can cause us to make errors that spoil the tactic's usefulness.

Below are three such errors. They might seem harmless, but each of them can lead to misleading tallies that are ultimately unreliable.

#1 - Compounding pros and cons

Because we intend to score each pro and con individually, it's important that we list them separately. If we unwittingly combine them, we risk assigning scores that fail to accurately represent their individual impact on us.

For example, suppose we mistakenly combined the following pros (from above) when deciding whether to invest $10,000:

- You'll save money for the future (5)
- You'll experience peace of mind that you have funds at your disposal (2)

Together, their individual scores total 7. If we had combined them (e.g. "You'll save money and therefore have peace of mind"), we might wrongly assign a value of 5. This will undermine the accuracy of our final tallies.

#2 - Duplicating pros and cons

This is a common error (I've done it myself). As we brainstorm the benefits and risks associated with a decision (Steps 2 and 3), we inadvertently restate one or more of them using different phrasing. This error will cause the repeated pro or con to receive undue weight during the scoring process (Step 4).

For example, we might unintentionally duplicate one of

the cons associated with investing $10,000 in the following manner:

- Your money will be at risk
- Your investment is not guaranteed

These two cons are essentially the same thing. They're just phrased differently. If we were to score each phrasing separately, we would give this particular con excessive weight, thereby weakening the validity of the final tallies.

#3 - Framing the decision to include multiple courses of action

This tactic is highly useful when we're deciding whether to take a particular course of action. It's far less useful when we incorporate multiple courses of action. Doing so blurs the associated pros and cons. They become less transparent.

Following is an example of proper framing of a decision:

Should I invest $10,000?

It highlights a single course of action. We either decide to move forward or abandon it. Here's an example of *improper* framing:

Should I invest $10,000 or use the money to build a home theater?

With two options in front of us, we've hampered our ability to create precise, clear lists of pros and cons. This will compromise our scoring and hurt the accuracy and reliability of our final tallies.

Again, the output of a weighted pros-and-cons list is only as good as the inputs. This tactic can be highly useful and actionable. But we must take great care in how we construct our lists.

LET's put the above into practice.

~

Exercise #7

~

LET's suppose you're thinking of buying a new laptop. Your current laptop still works, so a new model isn't necessary (if it were necessary, you wouldn't need a pros-and-cons list).

First, grab a blank piece of paper and create four columns as described above in Step 1. Make the first and third columns wider than the second and fourth columns.

Then, label them from left to right: Pros, Score, Cons, and
Score, respectively.

Second, think of every possible advantage associated
with buying a new laptop. Following are a few that might
be important to you (it's far from an exhaustive list):

- You won't need to worry about your laptop
  failing
- You'll be able to use the latest software
  and apps
- A new model will be more portable than your
  current model
- You'll have more storage capacity
- You'll enjoy better graphics

Third, brainstorm every possible disadvantage:

- You'll need to spend a significant amount of
  money
- You'll have to transfer a large number of files
  from your current laptop
- You'll be less familiar with the new model than
  your current one
- You might miss out on better models launching
  in the near future
- You may be forced to upgrade select software

Next, assign a score between 1 and 5 to each advantage

and disadvantage. The higher the score, the more important it is to you. Below, for illustrative purposes, I've scored the individual pros and cons according to their importance to me.

Pros:

- You won't need to worry about your laptop failing (5)
- You'll be able to use the latest software and apps (3)
- A new model will be more portable than your current model (3)
- You'll have more storage capacity (2)
- You'll enjoy better graphics (2)

Cons:

- You'll need to spend a significant amount of money (4)
- You'll have to transfer a large number of files from your current laptop (4)
- You'll be less familiar with the new model than your current one (3)
- You might miss out on better models launching in the near future (3)
- You may be forced to upgrade select software (3)

Lastly, tally the individual scores. I've done the math below.

Pros of buying a new laptop: 15
Cons of buying a new laptop: 17

By comparing the final tallies, we can immediately see that the disadvantages outweigh the advantages (at least for me). Therefore, I would decide to not buy a new laptop.

Note that we framed the decision as a choice between taking a defined course of action versus abandoning it (i.e. buy a new laptop vs do not buy a new laptop). If we had framed the decision with *multiple* courses of action (e.g. buy a new laptop vs buy a used laptop), we would have muddled the entire process. Doing so would have severely impaired the accuracy and usefulness of the final tallies.

Time required: 30 minutes

TACTIC #8: CREATE A DECISION CHECKLIST

Life is a matter of choices, and every choice you make makes you.

— JOHN C. MAXWELL

We sometimes have difficulty making big decisions because we're emotionally invested in the outcome or in select factors associated with our choices. This can lead us to make errors in judgment and overlook important variables.

A decision checklist is a tool that helps us to manage ourselves while making decisions. It keeps our emotions in check. By asking specific questions, we can more easily control our biases, prevent - or at least minimize - mistakes, and ultimately engineer the best possible outcomes given our circumstances.

Below, we'll discuss how decision checklists aid us in choosing between competing options and explore several best practices that'll optimize our results.

Decision Checklists 101

Numerous obstacles impede our ability to make effective decisions. On any given day, our attention is divided across multiple demands. Our energy levels wane as the day progresses. We're forced to put out small fires, preventing them from growing into full-blown emergencies. We're busy, tired, hungry, and sometimes in a bad mood. And then there are the cognitive biases that chip away at our ability to think rationally and logically.

It's no wonder we regularly make decisions that lead to disappointing results. The decision-making process becomes a blur in the busyness of our day.

Decision checklists bring into focus the critical factors associated with decisions. The questions we design direct our attention. They help us to concentrate on our priorities and suppress our cognitive biases. These questions also help to ensure we employ the same rules, benchmarks, and conventions throughout the decision-making process, and from one decision to the next. They promote *consistency*, which increases the predictability of our outcomes.

As with weighted pros-and-cons lists (Tactic #7), the value of a decision checklist's output is only as good as our inputs (the questions we design). So everything depends on asking the right questions.

There's no list of "correct questions." Every situation is unique. The questions we prepare should, naturally, address the most important variables involved in whatever decision we face.

For example, if the decision involves our business, some of the questions will likely address the availability of resources. If the decision regards our families or friends, some of the questions will probably take into account relational issues.

Creating effective decision checklists takes practice. The more you do them, the better you'll become at brainstorming questions that improve your decisions and lead to better outcomes. Fortunately, there are several simple techniques you can use to quickly scale the learning curve.

5 Best Practices for Creating Effective Decision Checklists

THESE BEST PRACTICES will help to ensure your questions are constructive and productive. None guarantee that your decision checklists will lead to superior choices and successful results. Nor will they make your decisions for you. But they *will* clarify your priorities, focus your attention on pivotal factors, and in the process highlight some you might otherwise overlook.

#1 - Start by listing your highest-priority considerations

It's helpful to use a "top-down" approach when brain-storming questions. Start with your highest-priority concerns and use them to flesh out the lower-priority ones. Begin this process by asking yourself "what are the 5 most important items I must consider when making this decision?"

Following is how such a list might appear if we were deciding how to invest $10,000:

1. investment objective (e.g. safety, growth, etc.)
2. age (the older you are, the less risk you'll likely tolerate)
3. other uses for the money (e.g. credit card debt, emergency fund, etc.)
4. risk tolerance (how much variability in your returns are you willing to endure?)
5. diversification (what mix of investment vehicles or asset categories is suitable for your circumstances?)

We can now use these five high-priority items to build our decision checklist. They'll serve as a guide as we come up with questions that bring to the foreground other considerations that matter to us.

#2 - Ask questions that can be answered with "yes" or "no"

This practice makes analysis of our options straightforward. It simplifies our decision-making by encouraging us to view individual variables through a binary lens. Each question has only two possible answers: "yes" or "no." And each answer provides further insight into the suitability of our options.

Following are a few "yes/no" questions we might ask to help us decide how to invest $10,000:

- Can I withstand a short-term negative return on my investment?
- Am I willing to keep the money invested for 10+ years?
- Does the fund manager have at least 10 years of experience (if we're considering investing in a mutual fund)?
- Can I liquidate my investment quickly if doing so becomes necessary?

This list can become extensive. But that's to our benefit. The longer our list of "yes/no" questions, the easier it will be for us to make a final decision. The reason will become clear with the third best practice.

#3 - Highlight questions that must be answered with "yes"

Recall the Go/No-Go Evaluation we discussed earlier (Tactic #6). That was a progressive decision-making model. We framed all of the factors that were relevant to our decision as "yes/no" questions and then considered them one by one. The decision to proceed or abandon the decision was based on an affirmative answer at each successive step.

Here, we'll do something similar. From our list of "yes/no" questions, highlight those that must be answered with "yes" in order for us to proceed. If you've written the questions on paper, simply outline them with a red pen. If you created your list digitally, rearrange it so these "deal-breaker" questions appear at the top.

Following are a few "dealbreaker" questions that might be attached to our decision regarding how to invest $10,000:

- Can I afford to lose a portion of my investment capital?
- Is this the most worthy use of my $10,000 at this time?
- Am I willing to leave my investment alone for at least 12 months?

These questions will vary based on our unique prefer-ences, concerns, and circumstances. Note that each one must be answered with a "yes." Depending on how we answer these questions, they will ultimately govern whether we decide to move forward with investing $10,000.

#4 - Check in with your emotions regarding the decision

This step may seem tangential to creating a decision checklist, but it's an integral component.

There's no way we can avoid our emotions. We shouldn't *try* to avoid them at all. As we discussed in the chapter *Why We Make Poor Decisions*, our emotions can help us to make healthy, productive choices. Problems arise when we fail to properly *manage* our emotions. With that in mind, we should monitor our emotional state and examine its soundness as we build our decision checklist. Doing so allows us to determine whether select emotions are hampering our progress.

Let's return to our "how to invest $10,000" example. Suppose we experience the following range of emotions as we decide whether and how to invest our money:

- fear
- anxiety
- panic
- optimism
- confidence
- greed
- frustration
- depression

Write them down. Then appraise each of them, one by one, and test their validity.

For example, it's natural for first-time investors to feel concerned about the safety of their money. But is it reasonable to experience anxiety or panic given the relative stability of the market over the past 100 years? Is the anxiety and panic valid? Likewise, it's natural for experienced investors to feel optimistic and confident when choosing investments. Here, we might ask whether we're feeling *overly* optimistic or *overly* confident in our ability to choose winning investments. Is our self-assurance reasonable?

Scrutinize the questions we've brainstormed thus far. Do any of them suggest an unproductive or fallacious emotional state regarding the matter at hand? For example, consider the following "dealbreaker" question:

Will I double my investment capital within three years?

This question suggests overoptimism. While it's possible for us to double our money in three years, it's not probable. Allowing our overoptimism, an unreasonable emotion, to dictate a dealbreaker question is unproductive. If we fail to keep it in check, we risk mistakenly abandoning the decision to invest at all.

#5 - Ask questions that highlight personal biases

We discussed noteworthy biases in the chapter *10 Cognitive Biases That Impact Our Decisions*. Here, we seek to detect them (they're not always obvious) and minimize their influence on our decision-making. We do so by asking questions designed specifically to reveal such biases.

For example, suppose we fear that confirmation bias might ruin our objectivity while we decide how to invest our money. We're pessimistic about the economy and every article we read reinforces this gloomy outlook. In this case we might ask the following questions:

- Have we gathered information and advice from sources outside the group upon which we normally rely?
- Have we rashly dismissed information and advice that challenged our presumptions?
- What alternative viewpoints have we failed to consider?

We should go through this process for each cognitive bias to which we're susceptible. Of course, doing so requires self-awareness. We must be aware of our biases before we can counteract them. *Part I: Understanding Our Decision-Making Process* will help to improve our recognition of them.

. . .

LET's put the above into practice.

∾

Exercise #8

∾

CONSIDER a big decision you're currently facing. There are undoubtedly numerous factors to consider, including certain emotions that may be attached to various options. Let's create a decision checklist using the best practices detailed above as a guide.

First, identify your top priorities relevant to the decision. For example, if the decision involves your career, these priorities may include compensation, the daily commute, and job satisfaction. If the decision concerns pursuing an advanced degree, your priorities might be tuition cost, scheduling concerns, and time to completion.

Now that we've identified the variables that matter most to us, let's create a list of relevant "yes/no" questions. These should stem from our top priorities. Here's a small sample regarding switching jobs:

- Does the new position come with a larger compensation package?
- Will my commute be longer if I accept the new position?

- Does the new company's culture align with my job-related passions and convictions?

Following is a small sample regarding pursuing an advanced degree.

- Can I pay for tuition without taking out loans?
- Will I be able to juggle my full-time job with doing assignments and taking exams?
- Can I acquire the degree within two years?

Use the above samples as a guide to brainstorm "yes/no" questions relevant to the decision you've chosen to investigate for this exercise.

Next, evaluate each of the "yes/no" questions you've brainstormed. Look for any that must be answered with a "yes" in order for you to proceed. Highlight them so they're easily identifiable.

In our "switching jobs" example, our dealbreaker question might be *"Does the new position come with a larger compensation package?"* In our "pursuing an advanced degree" example, our dealbreaker question may be *"Can I pay for tuition without taking out loans?"* If the answer is no, we immediately stop and abandon the decision.

Let's now acknowledge and address the emotions you're feeling regarding the decision. Are you excited? Do you feel sad or despondent? Are you struggling with worry and stress? Or do you feel optimistic and even joyful? It's also possible you're experiencing shame, confusion, and a sense of nostalgia.

Write these emotions down. Then analyze each one in light of the decision you face. Is the emotion reasonable and well grounded? Or is it baseless and unjustified? Note your conclusions next to the associated emotions.

Finally, identify the cognitive biases with which you've struggled in the past. Write them down. Then, brainstorm questions that reveal whether these select biases are harming your objectivity with respect to the decision at hand.

Time required: 30 minutes

TACTIC #9: CHALLENGE YOUR ASSUMPTIONS

❝ Making good decisions is a crucial skill at every level.

— PETER DRUCKER

Assumptions limit our frame of mind. They cause us to presuppose that certain options are infeasible or impractical.

On the one hand, assumptions serve as a protective measure. Our minds try to "fill in the blanks" when we're faced with the unknown. If we don't fully understand a situation, we assume things about it as a way to navigate the uncertainty.

The problem is, our assumptions are often inaccurate. Whether we make them about strangers, new places, or unfamiliar circumstances, we usually get things wrong. This habit can thus wreak havoc with our decision-making. If we make bad assumptions, we risk making terrible choices.

For this reason, we must always be willing to challenge our assumptions. We must regularly test them to check whether they can withstand scrutiny. Are they based on reliable data, information, and experience, or have we simply manufactured narratives to "fill in the blanks?"

Below, we'll go through the process of identifying our assumptions and evaluating them. It's a methodical, but relatively quick, procedure.

List Your Assumptions

Whether we recognize our assumptions depends on our self-awareness. Some of our beliefs are so deeply entrenched that they go unnoticed by us. Others are more conspicuous, but we avoid thinking about them because we know intuitively they are unsound or unfair.

The first step toward challenging our assumptions regarding a particular decision is to write them down. I recommend doing this on a blank sheet of paper rather than doing so digitally (i.e. on a laptop, phone, or tablet). Writing things down stimulates the brain. You may discover personal conjecture of which you were previously unaware. Additionally, you might immediately recognize illegitimate presumptions as you list them.

You may even instinctively challenge them. But doing so would be putting the proverbial cart before the horse.

For now, focus on identifying and listing the assumptions. Once we've completed the list, we'll appraise the credibility of each one by subjecting it to a series of seven simple tests.

7 Quick Ways to Challenge Your Assumptions

IT'S EASIER to test our assumptions if we rely on a system for doing so. If we challenge them haphazardly, we risk overlooking important benchmarks that should be met before we accept the assumptions as logical and defensible. With that in mind, following is a 7-step procedure for putting each of our assumptions through its paces.

#1 - Identify the source of the assumption

Perhaps it's a website. Maybe it's a physical publication. Possibly it's an individual whom you consider to be an expert on the matter. Or the assumption may stem from a past experience, a feeling in your gut, or a deeply-held belief system.

Write down the source.

This alone may reveal the assumption to be dubious. If the source is unreliable, so too may be the assumption.

#2 - Analyze the wording of the assumption

Wording matters. Some words and phrases provide too much latitude with regard to their interpretation. These include absolute qualifiers, such as "always" and "never." Using such words can broaden the scope of an assumption past the point of validity. For example, consider the following statement:

> "Investors always do well in bull markets."

This assumption is made false by its overly-broad wording. First, some investors are actually speculators. Second, the qualifier "always" hurts the assumption's credibility. The reality is, some individuals who put money into the market do poorly in bull markets.

This problem also manifests with words and phrases that provide too *little* latitude. Consider the following statement:

> "Stock investors can lose all of their investment capital."

This assumption is made false by its overly-*narrow* wording. To be sure, if we invest all of our money in a single stock and the company goes bankrupt, we may indeed lose everything. But the phrase "stock investors" implies a definition that's too restrictive. There are many ways to invest in stocks. Some vehicles, like mutual funds, offer a large degree of diversification that all but precludes a total loss.

#3 - Determine whether proof of the assumption exists

At its simplest level, an assumption is a hypothesis. Nothing more. It's unexamined and unproven. If we allow it to remain in this state, it can gain undeserved merit and influence our decisions. To nip this problem in the bud, we can apply the same investigative rigor to the assumption as we might to any other hypothesis.

Consider the basic 6-step scientific method:

1. Make an observation
2. Ask a question
3. Form a theory
4. Predict an outcome based on the theory
5. Test the prediction
6. Review the results

We don't have to go through this entire process. But it's worth doing steps 4 through 6 to verify the assumption is demonstrable and the expected results repeatable.

For example, recall our earlier assumption that *"investors always do well in bull markets."* All that is required to test this statement is to study past bull markets and look for evidence of poor results. Such results can occur due to investing at the top of the market (right before the inevitable downturn). It can also occur if an otherwise-balanced investment portfolio is adjusted so there's an over-allocation to high-risk growth stocks. Additionally, some sectors, such as utilities and healthcare, underperform during bull markets.

Ultimately, the statement *"investors always do well in bull markets"* can be easily proven false due to abundant evidence to the contrary.

#4 - Ask "what would happen if my assumption were proven wrong?"

First, suppose your assumption is incorrect. Now, ask yourself how things might transpire in light of this revelation.

How would you move forward? Would secondary speculations stem from this incorrect assumption? If so, can they too be ignored? And how might *that* affect your decision?

For example, let's say you've assumed that investing in the stock market carries a risk of total capital loss. This belief understandably makes you hesitant to invest. Now suppose this assumption is incorrect. Suppose there is zero possibility that you'll lose your entire stake. (Technically, this presumption is untrue. But such an outcome is highly implausible. Additionally, the presumption is merely for the purpose of this thought experiment.)

With the original assumption now deemed to be incorrect, how might that change your decision to invest? Would you now be more inclined to do so? Moreover, how might this revelation change the *manner* in which you invest? Would you now consider investment vehicles you had previously ruled out based on your original assumption?

This exercise shows how debunking an assumption can radically alter our perspective and choices. It reinforces the importance of rigorously testing our assumptions.

#5 - Imagine select components of the assumption were proven wrong

This step is an extension of step 4. Here, rather than supposing the assumption is *entirely* incorrect, we'll suppose that only *parts* of it are so. We'll modify select variables and evaluate how such changes might influence our decision-making.

Let's again suppose we're entertaining the following assumption:

> "Stock investors can lose all of their investment capital."

Rather than discarding this assumption outright, let's apply a few small modifications. Following are examples (with the changes in italics):

- "*Technology* stock investors can lose all of their investment capital."
- "*Cryptocurrency* investors can lose all of their investment capital."

- "Stock investors can lose a *significant portion* of their investment capital."
- "Stock investors can lose all of their investment capital *if we suffer another Great Depression.*"

How do these changes in the original assumption make you feel regarding the prospect of investing? As in Step 4, would you now be more inclined to do so? Would you consider investment vehicles you had previously ruled out?

By changing some of the parameters of an assumption, we can further scrutinize whether its influence on our decision-making is reasonable.

#6 - Lengthen the timeframe

Many of our assumptions stem from past experience. They arise from something that happened to us, usually within a short timeframe. Because they spring from experience, we believe them to be valid despite the fact that our perception is skewed.

For example, suppose you once invested $1,000 in a particular stock. Let's further suppose that you happened to invest this money mere days before the company announced lackluster financial results for the most recent quarter. The stock plummeted and you lost 30% of your capital. In a panic, you sold the shares and absorbed the loss.

This example experience happened within a short timeframe. Despite this fact, it now heavily influences your perception of investing in the stock market. Perhaps it has provided fuel to the assumption that investing in stocks is an overly-risky endeavor.

But let's lengthen the timeframe. Suppose you investigate the performance of this company's stock in the years prior to the most recent drop in its price. You find that it has endured such drops in the past and always fully recovered and subsequently *increased* in price. This new perspective, informed by a lengthened timeframe, hobbles our experience-based assumption that investing in stocks imposes excessive risk.

#7 - Introduce new information sources

We talked about information sources in Step 1. If a particular source is questionable, so too are all assumptions made from the information it provides.

Here, we introduce *new* sources. Rather than relying on our favorites, we seek sources that offer a fresh perspective. The information from these sources might contradict the information we obtain from our favorites. It may be unconventional or even seem radical.

This is to our benefit. Fresh viewpoints can help us debunk and ultimately discard incorrect assumptions.

For example, suppose we assume that investing in stocks carries excessive risk. This assumption has arisen, in large part, due to a few information sources upon which we rely. These sources are overtly pessimistic about the economy and cynical about stock investing in general.

Now suppose we introduce new information sources. These are more optimistic. They're bullish about the economy, strongly advocate the merits of investing in stocks, and support their position with reasonable justification. Exposure to these new information sources erodes the influence of the older, favored ones. In doing so, they whittle away at the undeserved credence we've given to the incorrect assumption.

LET's put the above into practice.

Exercise #9

FOR THIS QUICK EXERCISE, we're not going to address any particular decision you're facing. Instead, we'll focus on a single assumption that may be unduly influencing your outlook, choices, and behaviors. We'll scrutinize this assumption by applying the steps described above.

To start, select an unexamined belief or untested presumption that has great influence on your point of view. It might involve health care, education, or the environment. It may touch on specific inequalities or personal liberties. Choose one.

Now, let's put it through its paces.

First, make a list of the information sources that inform your position. Include websites, YouTube videos, and even friends, family members, and coworkers. Ask yourself whether these sources are experts on the subject matter. Any that are not can be disregarded without sacrificing the veracity of your position.

Second, examine how you typically word your assumption. Make note of absolute qualifiers (e.g. "never," "always," etc.). Look for overly-narrow wording that makes the assumption too restrictive to be true. Look for overly-broad wording that makes it too comprehensive.

Third, check whether the assumption is supported by incontrovertible proof. Is there evidence that counters the assumption? Are there exceptions that fall short of debunking it but still diminish its validity?

Fourth, imagine that you discover your assumption to be incorrect. How would that revelation affect you? How would it alter your perspective? Would you consider options you had previously dismissed? Would you feel that you enjoyed greater latitude in your choices?

Fifth, along the same lines as above, imagine that you learn certain elements of your assumption to be incorrect, or at least unreliable. The broad strokes may be valid, but the finer details are questionable. How would *that* finding influence you? How would *that* change your perspective? How might it expand your choices?

Sixth, stretch the timeframe of your assumption. If it was previously measured in days, lengthen it over several months. If it was previously measured in months, lengthen it over several years. Does the assumption still hold true? Does it have the same degree of validity? Or does lengthening the timeframe make the assumption less reliable?

Lastly, look for new information sources that address the subject matter surrounding the assumption. Specifically, seek conflicting views, dissenting opinions, and contrary evidence. Such sources can provide insightful counterpoints. If the assumption can survive them, you can be assured of its soundness. Otherwise, it may quickly become clear that the assumption is faulty.

Time required: 25 minutes

TACTIC #10: IGNORE THE SUNK COST FALLACY

 Once the decision is made, do not look back. Do not second guess your decisions.

— MUHAMMAD ALI

It's almost impossible to make good, rational decisions when we're worried about the money or time we've already spent. These past expenditures often cause us to feel obligated to commit to imprudent choices. We do so because we've already invested in them. We've already devoted resources to them. Abandoning them *feels* wrong to us.

So we end up staying the course. We remain committed even though we know intuitively that we're on the wrong path.

This is the sunk cost fallacy in action. It's a psychological trap that discourages us from cutting our losses and changing course, even when it makes good sense to do so.

As you can imagine, the sunk cost effect can ruin our decision-making. Below, we'll explore some examples of how it affects our decisions and discuss several tactics we can use to minimize its influence on us.

Examples of the Sunk Cost Effect on Our Decisions

Sunk costs are spent resources that cannot be retrieved. When this resource is money, examples include nonrefundable concert tickets, college tuition, and gym membership fees. The resource can also be time. Here, examples include watching movies, pursuing an advanced degree, or learning martial arts. In each of these cases, the spent resource, whether money or time, cannot be recouped.

Sunk costs are difficult for us to ignore. The investment of money or time creates an emotional attachment. We feel committed and become disinclined to let go. Additionally, many of us are unwilling to waste our resources. If we invest money or time toward a particular end, we want to ensure the investment is a worthwhile one. We have a natural aversion to cutting our losses.

For example, suppose you've bought tickets to a baseball game. You attend the event and it begins to drizzle during the fourth inning. You're miserable sitting exposed to the weather. But because the tickets are nonrefundable and you've already invested more than an hour in the game (plus travel time), you feel committed. So you decide to remain seated when leaving would arguably be the better option.

Or suppose you're attending university. You're halfway toward earning a degree in a field you've discovered that you dislike. So great is your distaste for the subject matter that you have no intention of working in this field following your graduation. But you've already invested a lot of time and money pursuing the degree. So you decide to stay the course. You continue to invest resources because your past expenditures make you feel obligated to do so. Your decision has been unduly influenced by the sunk cost effect.

One more example: suppose you're in an unhealthy friendship. Your friend treats you poorly, provides no emotional support when you're in need of it, and the two of you argue whenever you're together. Despite no longer enjoying your friend's company, you decide to continue the friendship. After all, you've invested years of your life into it. Abandoning the friendship seems wrong even though it may have outlived its purpose. Here, the optimal decision may be to simply end the friendship. Unfortunately, the sunk cost effect encourages you to perpetuate it.

We've all fallen prey to the sunk cost fallacy at some point. We've all made poor decisions based on past investments of our money, time, and other resources. Let's take a look at some ways we can prevent doing so in the future.

5 Simple Tactics to Overcome the Sunk Cost Fallacy

WE MUST OVERCOME the bias toward throwing good resources after bad if we hope to make healthy, effective decisions. This tendency may be deeply ingrained in many of us, often without our realization. The good news is, it's relatively easy to counter by employing a few simple practices.

#1 - Consider the opportunity costs

When we continue to devote resources toward endeavors stemming from previous decisions, we often develop tunnel vision. We focus exclusively on whether our current efforts are producing a net gain. If they are, we stay the course.

But this perspective ignores the attendant opportunity costs. The resources we are devoting to our current activities cannot be used for *other* activities.

For example, suppose we are investing $1,000 each month into a particular mutual fund. The fund ends up losing money. Let's also suppose that we convince ourselves that selling our shares will only serve to lock in our losses (we're falling victim to the sunk cost effect). So we continue to put money into the fund each month, hopeful it'll eventually recoup its losses.

Here, we're ignoring the opportunity costs associated with the ongoing investment. For instance, suppose we are also carrying $20,000 in credit card debt. This debt is accompanied by a 15% interest rate. Even if our mutual fund manages to recoup its losses and keep pace with the market (i.e. appreciate at 8% to 10% each year), we'll still suffer a net loss. If we ignore this opportunity cost (paying off the debt rather than investing), we risk overlooking this perpetual loss.

If you're seeing poor results stemming from a decision and staying the course simply because you've already invested a lot of time and money, think about the opportunity costs.

#2 - Sever any personal attachment to the decision

Sometimes we become emotionally attached to our decisions. Doing so makes it difficult for us to cut our losses and change course. This is a slightly different manifestation of the sunk cost effect.

Such attachments can stem from a personal interest in the matter. An example would be buying a new vehicle we love despite learning that it has a reputation for engine problems.

Attachments can also spring from a sense of obligation. We commit emotionally to an endeavor and feel compelled to see it through to the end. An example would be refusing to abandon a terrible film because we feel connected to the main actor due to his roles in films we've enjoyed. The greater our emotional attachment, the more difficult it is for us to abandon the endeavor.

One way to counter this sunk cost effect is to proactively sever our emotional attachments to the decision in question. We should ask ourselves:

- "What is the worst that can happen if we abandon this project?"
- "What would failure look like?"
- "How might this failure affect our future prospects?"

Answering these questions dampens the irrational fears they inspire when they're left unexamined. We may find that walking away from a project arising from a previous decision has no lasting impact on us. If that's the case, walking away may be the best, most productive option despite the resources we've invested.

#3 - View previous decisions as non-binding on future decisions

This practice effects a simple change in mindset. When we make decisions, we feel a sense of commitment to them. And every successive decision regarding that particular endeavor reinforces that sentiment. As noted above, the greater our feeling of commitment, the harder it is for us to let go. This can cause us to stick to unwise, unproductive decisions and disregard superior options that are contrary to our original choices.

For example, suppose we've decided to invest $10,000 into a mutual fund. We have yet to select a fund. We've merely decided to invest in one. We've made the initial decision, and our level of commitment remains relatively low.

But suppose we decide to take the next step: researching viable options. We spend significant time comparing various funds' performance records. Through this effort, we've deepened our level of commitment.

Next, suppose we've finally selected a mutual fund and decided to take the next logical step: opening an account. We complete the necessary paperwork online; we provide personal details (name, social security number, etc.) along with our bank account information.

Notice how each subsequent decision reinforces our commitment to invest $10,000 into this mutual fund. We almost feel obligated to do so. We've spent so much time pursuing *this* option that we all but ignore other options (e.g. using the money to pay off our credit cards). It's another example of the sunk cost effect.

We can avoid this trap by recognizing that our previous choices impose no obligation to follow a particular course of action. Such choices are non-binding on us. This concession gives us the confidence to walk away from a decision when doing so becomes sensible. We learn to cut our losses rather than stay the course based on a false sense of obligation.

#4 - Focus on data rather than emotion

As noted above, we often get emotionally attached to our decisions. This is problematic because it makes us disinclined to entertain options that oppose these decisions. We may even become defensive when we're presented with information that contradicts the reasoning we used to make them.

When this occurs, the limbic system of our brain, the part that handles our emotions, begins to reinforce the sunk cost effect. The stronger the connection between our emotional state and our previous decisions, the more difficult it becomes for us to abandon them.

Here, the solution is simple. We must get into the habit of prioritizing data over our emotions. We must rely on dispassionate information rather than our gut feelings. Only then can we rationally determine the wisdom and practicality of our options, particularly those that run counter to our current course of action.

This takes practice. The only way to develop this habit is by doing it over and over. To that end, whenever you're about to make a decision that perpetuates your current course of action ask yourself "does the data support this decision?"

#5 - Ask yourself whether your ego is at stake

Sometimes, all signs indicate that we should abandon a particular course of action, but we hold on because of our ego. We might feel that we made the right decisions and are now loathe to admit we were wrong. We may actually be convinced that our decisions will ultimately yield good results even as the situation becomes untenable.

Our ego can easily become the perfect bedfellow to the sunk cost fallacy. As noted, the more resources we invest into a decision, the greater our emotional attachment to it. Our self-worth becomes entwined with the results of our choices. It can reach the point that we're unable to let go even as our initial decisions are proven to be misguided.

To prevent this situation, we must divorce our ego from our decision-making. First, we must acknowledge that we sometimes make unwise choices, and doing so is neither a reflection of our intelligence nor competence. Second, we must get into the habit of asking ourselves whether we're catering to our ego when we're about to make a decision.

For example, suppose you've told friends and family members that you intend to invest $10,000 into a particular stock. You're absolutely convinced it's a good investment based on your research, and have praised your investment prowess for having discovered it. Before you actually invest in this stock, ask yourself "is my ego at stake?" If the answer is "yes," it's worth reevaluating the decision to ensure it still makes sense.

LET's put the above into practice.

Exercise #10

CONSIDER a decision with which you're currently struggling. Maybe you're about to purchase a new vehicle. Perhaps you're considering moving to a different state. Or you might be thinking about changing careers. We're going to put this decision through the gauntlet by asking ourselves a series of pointed questions.

First, brainstorm the opportunity costs associated with this decision. What options become unavailable to you if you move forward? What opportunities will you forego? Write them down. Be exhaustive. Then, ask yourself the following questions:

- Am I willing to sacrifice everything on my list?
- Will I be happy going without the things on my list?

If the answer to either question is "no," you should abandon the decision.

If your decision survives the first step, identify any personal attachments you have with it. Ask yourself the following questions:

- Why is this decision important to me?
- What's the worst that can happen if I walk away from it?

- How might walking away affect my future?

Your answers may reveal that you're inclined to move forward due solely to the resources you've invested up to this point (sunk cost effect).

Next, recognize that your previous decisions regarding the matter at hand do not obligate you to stick with the endeavor. Ask yourself the following questions:

- Given that my previous decisions are non-binding, what is my reason for moving forward?
- Am I still convinced my choices will produce good results? Or am I moving forward simply because I feel compelled to do so by my previous choices?

Next, consider whether your emotions are playing a role in your decision-making process. Ask yourself the following questions:

- What is motivating me to make this decision?
- Why do I feel emotionally attached to this course of action?
- Does the data in front of me support choosing this option given my goals and priorities?

Finally, determine whether your ego is involved in the decision. If it is, you risk making a terrible choice for dubious reasons. Ask yourself the following questions:

- How would I feel admitting I was wrong to consider this decision?
- Would I feel embarrassed if I decide to walk away?
- Do I feel jealous of others who have made a similar decision?

If, after completing this exercise, you're still convinced that moving forward with a particular course of action is a wise decision, it likely is. At the very least, you can rest assured that you're moving forward sensibly and purposefully rather than because you've fallen victim to the sunk cost fallacy.

Time required: 20 minutes

TACTIC #11: IDENTIFY AND AVOID INFORMATION OVERLOAD

 We live in a world where there is more and more information, and less and less meaning.

— JEAN BAUDRILLARD

W e need facts, figures, and other forms of information to make effective decisions. Without them, we're forced to blindly follow our gut feelings and intuition. So a critical part of making healthy, productive, *rational* choices is searching for - and acquiring - reliable information.

Having said that, it's possible to have too much of a good thing. While reliable information is indispensable to the decision-making process, it can also become a detriment. Too much can overwhelm us. It's possible to become

so inundated with information that we become paralyzed
with indecision.

This is information overload in a nutshell.

How Information Overload Happens (and How It Harms the Decision-Making Process)

We have access to more information at our fingertips than
at any time in history. The internet allows us to obtain
details about every subject imaginable within seconds.
With a few hours of research, we can obtain more information than we can possibly use. We can advance from a
state of ignorance to one of enlightenment on any topic we
desire.

This *seems* like a boon. But it can easily become a
burden, particularly when we're trying to sort through
multiple options and select the best one.

Information overload occurs when the volume of
incoming data exceeds our ability to process it. The information becomes unmanageable.

Ideally, our brains would simply cut off the flow of
incoming information when we have enough to make an
effective decision. But that is rarely what happens. Instead,
the flood of information, which often leads to an ever-
expanding set of options (most of which are impractical or
untenable), causes a cognitive short circuit. Our brains shut
down. The volume of information exceeds our processing
ability.

We're susceptible to information overload for a few

simple reasons. First, a massive volume of new information is created each day. Second, we feel naturally compelled to obtain as much information as possible before we make important decisions. Third, most of us lack systems for processing the information we acquire. We lack a workable method for filtering, organizing, and evaluating it.

This usually results in one of two situations. On the one hand, we suffer analysis paralysis. We become unable to move forward with a decision. We fear making the wrong choice, feeling we haven't sufficiently analyzed the relevant details.

Or we become exasperated with our predicament. Faced with an unmanageable mountain of information, we ignore it all in frustration and make an impulsive, reckless decision based on our gut feeling.

Clearly, neither situation accommodates rational, productive decision-making. So let's develop a system that helps us to avoid both of them.

A Simple 4-Step System to Avoid Information Overload

THE GOOD NEWS IS, it's easy to avert information overload. All that's required is a actionable methodology that allows us to identify the information we need, filter the stuff we *don't* need, and quickly organize and process the former.

This may sound like a colossal undertaking. But it's simpler than you might imagine. The following 4-step system will all but ensure that you avoid information over-load when making important decisions.

Step #1: Streamline incoming information

Most of the information we encounter will be unhelpful to us. Some of it will be irrelevant. Some of it will be inapplicable. And some of it may be relevant, but so expansive that it offers little practical value.

So the first step is to create a method for filtering low-value information and obtaining high-value information. To do so, we need to consider the following two factors:

1. *Type of information.* This can include current events about the subject matter surrounding a decision. It may involve product specifications, pending legislation, or available applications. The type of information we need will depend on the nature of the decision we face (e.g. business, consumer, personal, etc.).
2. *Sources of information.* This might involve research websites that offer scholarly papers for a fee. It may also include online databases, news media sites, blogs, and even social media for opinions from subject matter experts. We might also find value in physical publications, such as academic books or select trade magazines.

Once we've identified the *type* of information we need,

along with the sources that offer it, we'll need an efficient way to organize it.

Step #2: Develop a method for judging the priority of content

It's easy to fall into the trap of reading without purpose. We first obtain a mountain of relevant information. But rather than prioritizing it, we simply dive in. We treat every piece of content equally, poring over each piece without regard for whether it truly deserves our time and attention.

This approach wastes time. Worse, it dulls our appreciation for the details that carry the greatest impact. By treating all acquired information with the same priority, we risk overlooking the truly actionable stuff. Let's create a method that allows us to avoid this problem.

First, quickly inspect each piece of information and assign it a priority level 1, 2, or 3. The highest priority level (1) should be reserved for content that promises actionable details. The second-highest priority level (2) should signify content that is informative, but not directly actionable. The lowest priority level (3) should represent content that seems interesting, but is neither informative nor actionable.

Second, assign each piece of information into one of three groups: browse, read, or study. Once we've done so, here's how we'll tackle the content in each group:

Browse - We'll read titles and subtitles. We'll take heed of numbered and bulleted lists. We'll perform keyword searches on particular phrases relevant to our decision.

Read - We'll read the content from beginning to end.

Study - In addition to reading the content, we'll take notes. These notes may include details for conducting further research. They might also include summaries of critical information and comments regarding how we can take action on it.

It's tempting to assume we can assign each piece of content we've obtained into one of the above three groups (browse, read, or study) according to each piece's priority level. But that won't always be the case. Some high-priority content can be browsed based on its format. Some low-priority content may warrant a complete read-through (and possibly note-taking), especially if it's brief.

The third and final step is to decide when to read each piece of information. Again, it's tempting to assume we should tackle the high-priority content first and leave the low-priority content for last. But our decision should be based on the following factors:

- the ease with which we can consume the content
- the time required to consume it
- how quickly we can take action on it

If we can consume a piece of information quickly, it might make sense to do so sooner rather than later, even if we've assigned it a low-priority level. It may contain an interesting detail we can use. Conversely, we might reasonably postpone reading a high-priority article because it's lengthy, comprehensive, and demands focus.

We've now successfully created a system to help us prioritize the information we've acquired. Let's discuss how to filter some of the content that's likely to cross our desks.

Step #3: Filter low-relevance information

Low-relevance information is content that doesn't help us move forward with our current decision. It may be pertinent to some of our other projects or responsibilities. But it's unrelated to the decision we're currently struggling with. Such content can include the following:

- emails from coworkers, customers, bosses, friends, family members.
- peer-reviewed articles
- trade magazines
- scholarly journals
- financial reports
- survey results
- current news
- website articles

We need to use filters to prevent low-relevance content

from taking away our time and attention from high-relevance content. Following are a few simple filters we can easily put into place:

Email filters

Most email providers (Gmail, Outlook, Yahoo Email, etc.) allow you to set filters based on various parameters. Set a filter that highlights emails that contain words and phrases relevant to your decision in the email's subject line or body. The highlight will make these emails stand out among the rest.

If you currently receive a large volume of email that doesn't require your immediate attention, set filters that automatically put them into folders for later review. You can do this based on words and phrases found in the email's subject line or body. Alternatively, if a sender's emails exclusively address a particular topic, filter them based on the sender's email address. Send them to a folder with the sender's name so you can easily find them later.

Time-required filters

If you can fully consume a piece of relevant information within 60 seconds, do so immediately rather than filing it away. Filing it, retrieving it later, and then reading it increases the handling of the information. It also creates a backlog. If you have lots of small pieces of unread content filed away, they'll end up taking more time and requiring more effort down the road.

Productivity consultant David Allen, author of *Getting Things Done*, advocates a similar time-required filter. He refers to it as the "2-minute rule." Allen suggests that if something can be done within two minutes, and it'll require *more* than two minutes for handling and reflection later, do it now. It'll boost your efficiency.

Use this same approach when filtering information.

Delegation filters

You'll sometimes receive content that requires action, but isn't directly associated with the decision you're wrestling with. In such cases, it may be possible to delegate the content, along with the required action, to others.

For example, suppose a coworker emails you regarding a report for which your department is responsible. Your coworker asks you to provide a estimated completion date. Rather than shifting your focus away from perusing content relevant to an important decision, forward the email to someone in your group and ask that individual to respond in your stead.

Or suppose you're planning a family vacation. You and your spouse have chosen a destination. You're responsible for booking the travel package and accommodations and your spouse has agreed to plan the daily itinerary. If you run across content regarding local restaurants, kid-friendly activities, or interesting excursions, forward it to your spouse. Delegate it so you can focus on choosing flights with minimal stopovers along with a well-reviewed, conveniently-located hotel.

Routine-based filters

Some types of information can be filtered based on your routine. For example, suppose you receive a trade magazine that contains an article that'll prove useful in making an important decision. Let's also suppose that part of your daily routine is to read trade magazines while eating lunch. In this case, you can set aside the magazine in accordance with your established routine.

This type of filter can be applied toward email, online research, or even when seeking advice from others. If you already have a routine in place, use it as a filtering tool to organize and manage incoming information.

Step #4: Set time limits

In Step #3, we talked about time-required filters. That was in the context of consuming small chunks of relevant information quickly (i.e. if we can read it within one minute, we should do it now rather than later). We can use a similar approach to process *all* of the information that we come across.

Here, we set time limits on each piece of information. These time limits prevent us from spending an inordinate amount of time on any specific piece.

For example, suppose you've set aside a trade article to read while eating lunch. It's a long article, and you could potentially spend your entire lunch break reading it. Let's also suppose you intend to consume other content during your lunch break, so you can't spend the entire break reading this single article.

Set a time limit. Give yourself 30 minutes to read the article. Set a timer on your phone that alerts you when the 30 minutes have elapsed. When the timer goes off, move on to the next piece of content you had planned to read during your lunch break.

We can counter Parkinson's Law with this approach. Parkinson's Law states that "work expands so as to fill the time available for its completion." If you neglect to set a time limit, you might inadvertently spend your entire lunch break reading the long trade article. Consequently, you'd be forced to postpone reading the other content. Setting a time limit prevents this problem.

LET's put the above into practice.

∼

Exercise #11

∼

FOR PREVIOUS EXERCISES, we took into account decisions you might currently be facing. That approach is unnecessary here. For this exercise, we can address any subject matter for which you have an ongoing interest. This might include politics, social issues, or a particular hobby (e.g. cooking, golf, playing the guitar, etc.). Pick one for which you regularly consume a large volume of content and are thus at risk of suffering information overload.

First, let's streamline the incoming information. We'll identify each piece's *type* and *source*. This will help us to organize and prioritize it.

For example, suppose you regularly consume content regarding cooking. You watch videos on Youtube; you read books that teach cooking techniques; you peruse blogs that show how to prepare specific recipes; you receive numerous email newsletters regarding cooking; you're a member of several Reddit groups that focus on cooking. Write down these types of information along with their respective sources.

Second, we'll prioritize each piece of information based on its usefulness. Let's assign a 1, 2, or 3 to signify the priority level of each piece.

For example, suppose the cooking channels you follow on Youtube offer content that's actionable rather than simply informational. You've saved 20 videos to your queue and plan to watch them over the next couple weeks. Scan the list and assign a 1, 2, or 3 to each video according to the immediacy of its usefulness. For instance, if you need to watch a video to prepare tonight's meal, you would assign that video a 1. If a video is interesting, but not immediately useful, assign it a 2 or 3.

At this point, we'd normally determine whether we should browse, read, or study a particular piece of information. Instructional videos usually need to be consumed in their entirety. So let's move on to deciding when to watch the videos.

Recall from earlier that our decision should be based on the following criteria:

- the ease with which we can consume the content
- the time required to consume it
- how quickly we can take action on it

A 10-minute instructional cooking video may take priority over a 60-minute video because it's less intensive (ease of consumption). It might take priority simply because we can get through it more quickly. It may take priority because we can put the information to immediate use while the longer video might require more contemplation and preparation.

Third, set up filters that help us to manage low-relevance information. Recall the four types of filters discussed earlier:

1. email filters
2. time-required filters
3. delegation filters

4. routine-based filters

Email filters can be used to manage the cooking-related email newsletters to which you're subscribed. Time-required filters can be employed to handle small pieces of content and prevent a backlog. Delegation filters won't be of much use here since cooking is mostly a solitary activity. But routine-based filters *can* be useful. Decide when to watch cooking videos, read cooking-related books, blogs, and newsletters, and wade through cooking Reddit groups based on your daily routine.

Now, the fourth and final step: set time limits. For example, give yourself 30 minutes to scan the cooking Reddit groups you follow. Allow 45 minutes to read the email newsletters you receive. Limit the time you spend on cooking-related blogs to 25 minutes. Set a timer to keep yourself on track.

Time required: 30 minutes

TACTIC #12: USE MENTAL MODELS TO MAKE BETTER CHOICES

> Truly successful decision making relies on a balance between deliberate and instinctive thinking.
>
> — MALCOLM GLADWELL

Mental models are extremely useful tools that have myriad applications. Entire books have been written explaining how to develop and use them in every aspect of our lives.

This chapter will focus exclusively on how mental models can be used to improve our decision-making. I'll define what they are and explain how they're beneficial to the process of making healthy, productive, and rational choices. We'll then take a look at five specific mental models that will prove to be valuable aids when you're making important decisions.

What Is a Mental Model?

At its core, a mental model is a specific way of thinking about something. It's a lens through which we perceive the world around us and better understand how it works. Mental models can help us to solve problems, contemplate issues, identify opportunities, and establish causal connections. They help us to think better, improve our investigative ability, avoid blind spots, and make wiser, more productive decisions.

Numerous models are available to us. We should adopt, practice, and use several whenever we make weighty decisions. As noted by Charlie Munger, Vice Chairman of Berkshire Hathaway, Inc., we need a "latticework" of mental models to ably deconstruct and solve problems that challenge us.

How Do Mental Models Improve Decision-Making?

Our decisions are only as effective as our ability to correctly perceive the issues and circumstances that surround them. If we make choices without properly understanding the issues at stake, we risk making poor choices. If we fail to notice the causal connections between inputs and outputs, we risk making choices that lead to undesirable, and entirely avoidable, outcomes. If we perceive issues through a limited or biased lens, we risk misinterpreting the information that's supposed to *help* us make good decisions.

Mental models help us to steer clear of these problems. Applying the appropriate model allows us to expand our understanding of a particular situation and develop constructive theories that support and encourage wise decisions. It helps us to better comprehend our circumstances and focus on the variables that have the greatest impact.

For example, the science of economics is often murky and confusing. But we can use various mental models, such as supply and demand, comparative advantage, and marginal utility, to better understand particular economic issues. Likewise, physics is a subject that goes over the heads of many of us (myself included). Yet, we can use a plethora of mental models, such as inertia, thermodynamics, and relativity to better comprehend factors that affect specific outcomes.

Mental models aren't just useful for the sciences. We can develop models that help us to more ably interpret problematic situations in every area of our lives, from our relationships to our jobs. Once we develop the correct models, we can use them to make better decisions.

5 Mental Models That Will Help You to Make Better Decisions

THERE ARE thousands of mental models we can use to better understand the world around us. Most of them have limited application, especially in the context of productive decision-making. But there are several that will prove useful to us. Below, we'll explore five mental models that will do much of the heavy lifting for us when we need to make important decisions.

#1 - First Principles

We're regularly faced with complex problems. Normally, we're able to navigate them by relying on our values, belief systems, experience, and assumptions. Or we emulate others' decisions and behaviors when they're faced with similar circumstances.

Sometimes, however, the problems and decisions we face introduce factors that make these tools obsolete. We therefore have to use a different approach. First-principles reasoning encourages us to break down an issue to the point that we no longer make assumptions about it. From there, rather than thinking about the issue in terms of our constraints, we think about it in terms of the possibilities.

For example, consider how young children constantly ask "why" when they're faced with a statement:

Parent: "You need to go to bed."
Child: "Why?"
Parent: "Because you need sleep."
Child: "Why?"

Parent: "Because without sleep, you'll feel tired tomorrow."

Child: "Why?"

Parent: "Because the brain requires sleep to function properly."

Child: "Why?"

And so on.

Children, by nature, think of issues through the lens of first-principles reasoning. Yes, it can be aggravating for parents. But it's a good example of how to use this tool to better understand the circumstances surrounding a particular decision or issue.

#2 - Inversion

We usually approach issues from the perspective of what we'd like to accomplish. We base our actions, behaviors, and choices on our desired results. We establish a goal, create an action plan, and proceed through it step by step.

This approach is provably effective. But it's not always sufficient when we face complex issues. Sometimes, it's useful to approach issues in the opposite manner. Rather than thinking about our desired outcome and pondering how to achieve it, we consider the potential setbacks and fiascos and contemplate how to avoid them. Essentially, we think *backward* rather than forward.

The aforementioned Charlie Munger once quipped,

"All I want to know is where I'm going to die, so I'll never go there." That's inversion in a nutshell.

Thinking backward about a problem doesn't come easily to most of us. We have to develop the habit through practice. The upside is, if we train ourselves to think both forward and backward about issues, we can better identify avoidable errors as well as opportunities we might otherwise overlook.

For example, suppose we want to invest $10,000 into stocks. We instinctively think about our desired outcome: capital appreciation. This mindset leads us to consider stocks that have recently performed well. But let's "invert" this issue. Let's think backward about it. Instead of focusing on our desired outcome, we'll focus on a potential setback: capital *depreciation.* How do we avoid losing money? One way is to identify stocks selling at prices lower than their intrinsic value.

Incidentally, this strategy is referred to as "value investing." It has been used to great effect by Munger and his partner Warren Buffet. And it has its roots in the inversion mental model.

#3 - Occam's Razor

You've no doubt heard of Occam's Razor. You may already subscribe to the principle. It is simultaneously one of the simplest and most useful mental models available to us. When applied properly, it can help us to peel away the complexities of a problem, get to the heart of the matter, and resolve it with efficiency.

The philosopher William of Ockham stated (in Latin in the 1300s) that "plurality should not be posited without necessity." This statement has been altered slightly over the last 800 years to "the simplest explanation is usually the best one." Essentially, if we're faced with a confusing problem and presented with a complicated explanation and a simple one, the latter is usually more reliable than the former.

Let's return to our "invest $10,000" example. Suppose we're uncertain how to invest our money given the myriad investment vehicles available to us. Should we buy stocks? Should we write options? Should we use technical analysis to identify and exploit inefficiencies in the market? What about bonds? And if we decide to invest in bonds, what type should we consider (municipals, high-yield bonds, corporate bonds, Treasuries, etc.)? It can quickly become a complicated issue.

By using Occam's Razor, we can cut through the unnecessary complexities and focus on a simpler solution: index funds. Index funds tend to keep pace with the market while most other investment vehicles fail to do so over time. Occam's Razor thus simplifies our decision regarding how to invest $10,000.

Occam's Razor isn't a foolproof mental model. Far from it, in fact. But it's a highly useful one, particularly when complex issues cause us to fall victim to indecision and analysis paralysis.

#4 - Second-Order Thinking

Everyone practices *first*-order thinking, even if they do so without realizing it. First-order thinking is the recognition of immediate consequences. If we strike someone in anger, we can expect an angry response. If we're lactose intolerant and eat a large bowl of ice cream, we can expect digestive distress. If we go to bed at night without setting an alarm, we can expect to oversleep the following morning.

Second-order thinking forces us to consider the subsequent effects of our decisions. It encourages us to ask "what happens next?" For example, if we strike someone in anger, what happens following this individual's angry response? Will he call the police? Will he enlist the help of his friends to respond in kind? If we're in a public venue, will my party be asked to leave?

If we go to bed at night without setting an alarm, what happens after we oversleep the following morning? Will we miss an important meeting at work? Will we fail to get our children ready for school on time? Will we be forced to skip breakfast in the rush to recoup lost time?

We can take second-order thinking to the nth degree. For example, third-order thinking would consider "what happens next" if the person we assaulted calls the police. Will we be taken to jail? And if so, would we then be saddled with a police record? How might that impact our employment opportunities in the future? In the case of oversleeping and consequently missing an important work-related meeting, would we then be fired? And if so, would that affect our ability to pay the mortgage on our home? What happens if we lose our home in this manner?

Second-order thinking is a powerful mental model. It can help us to make better decisions by revealing potential consequences we'd otherwise overlook. Billionaire investor and hedge fund manager Ray Dalio once noted:

> Failing to consider second- and third-order consequences is the cause of a lot of painfully bad decisions.

This mental model can be extremely beneficial to us in every area of our lives. It can inform all of our decisions, from the trivial to the consequential, giving us a broader perspective with which to make wiser, healthier, and more productive choices.

#5 - Probabilistic Thinking

We often make decisions without having a full grasp of our circumstances. We focus on the *possibility* of certain outcomes that stem from our choices. Probabilistic thinking encourages us to consider the *probability* of these outcomes. That is, how likely are these possible outcomes to occur?

This mental model makes heavy use of math and logic to estimate odds. A comprehensive review of it would involve discussion of Bayesian philosophy, distribution curves, and topics like Markov logic networks, evidentiary reasoning, and argumentation theory. These subjects extend far beyond our purposes.

We can boil down probabilistic thinking with regard to everyday decision-making as follows: the *possibility* of an outcome is less useful to us in making a decision than the *probability* of that same outcome.

For example, suppose we're thinking of buying a stack of lottery tickets. It's possible that we'll win a large sum of money. But this outcome is highly improbable. Here, the possibility of winning shouldn't influence our decision to buy the lottery tickets. When we consider the infinitesimal odds of winning, we might reasonably decide against the purchase.

Like most mental models, probabilistic thinking isn't foolproof. We can differentiate between possible outcomes and probable outcomes, and still make ill-fated decisions. But practicing this manner of thinking gives us a better, more useful perspective.

LET's put the above into practice.

∾

Exercise #12

∾

LET'S use our "invest $10,000" example for this exercise. It's merely a proxy, of course. If you're currently struggling with an important decision, I encourage you to use *that* in place of my investment example.

(Note: this is the most time-intensive exercise in this book. But it's worth completing as it demonstrates a highly-useful tactic for making better decisions.)

As we have in previous examples, let's suppose we're considering investing $10,000. We're aware of the available investment vehicles (e.g. stocks, bonds, mutual funds, options, etc.). And we have a clear goal: long-term capital appreciation. It's now a matter of choosing an investment vehicle that best accommodates this goal.

First, let's examine our intention to invest by applying first principles reasoning (mental model #1 above). Doing so will either reinforce our intention or reveal it to be ill-advised. Here's how our use of this mental model might progress:

Us: "I need to invest $10,000."

First-principles reasoning (FPR): Why?

Us: "To grow our money."

FPR: Why do you want to grow your money?

Us: "To save for the future."

FPR: Why do you want to save for the future?

Us: "I want to live comfortably without worrying about money."

FPR: Is investing the only way to do this?

Us: "No. I can put the money into a bank savings account. Or under my bed mattress."

FPR: Why not pursue those options?

Us: "Because the money won't grow as quickly.

This is, of course, a simplistic application of the first-principles reasoning. But it demonstrates how this mental model allows us to break down problems to their most basic components.

Next, let's apply inversion (mental model #2 above). Here, we'll focus on the opposite of what we'd like to accomplish by investing $10,000. We'll think backwards about the issue. We start by asking ourselves *"What outcomes do we want to avoid?"* Following are a few potential answers:

- We lose all of our money.
- We lose a significant portion of our money.
- Our investment undergoes huge spikes and slumps (high volatility).
- Our investment underperforms the market year after year.
- We're unable to access our money when we need it.

By asking this question, we gain a better understanding of the issue, the stakes involved, and the associated risks. Indeed, our answers might rule out some of the available options (e.g. investing in options and futures, penny stocks, and junk bonds.).

Next, let's apply Occam's Razor (mental model #3 above). We did much of the heavy lifting earlier with regard to the problem of investing $10,000. But let's review.

We recognized that we have many options available to us. In fact, there are so many investment vehicles that choosing from among them is difficult. Applying Occam's Razor simplifies the decision.

The potential of an investment vehicle isn't directly correlated with the complexity of its design. It's possible to achieve our goal (capital appreciation) and avoid the undesirable outcomes we identified by applying inversion without becoming mired in complicated investment schemes. For example, by using Occam's Razor, we recognize that index funds can perform just as well as reverse convertibles, currency plays, and various derivative-based investments. Along with inversion, this mental model can help us to significantly whittle down our list of options.

Next, let's apply second-order thinking (mental model #4 above) to our decision to invest $10,000. We'll start with the first-order decision and ask "what happens next?" to identify potential second-order outcomes.

For example, suppose we've identified a company that has posted multiple quarters of rosy financials. Rather than immediately buying the stock, we ask ourselves "what happens next?" One possible answer is that the company attracts a lot of attention from other investors. These investors buy the stock in droves, causing its price to rise far above its intrinsic value. The stock thus becomes overpriced and susceptible to a downturn. In this scenario, a promising investment now looks far less promising. Second-order thinking could prevent us from making a costly mistake.

Lastly, let's apply probabilistic thinking (mental model #5 above). Consider the many investment options available to us:

- stocks
- bonds
- mutual funds
- options
- annuities
- commodities
- currencies
- cryptocurrencies
- real estate
- money-market funds

Each option carries the *possibility* of capital appreciation. But this knowledge is all but useless to us. First, it's also possible that we'll lose money (suffer capital depreciation). Second, this "knowledge" ignores the magnitude of potential capital appreciation as well as the time required for it to occur.

To make a wise decision regarding how to invest our $10,000, we need to assess the *probability* of specific outcomes. For example, suppose we want our investment to grow by 8% each year. Let's also suppose that we want to achieve this goal with low volatility. What are the odds that investing in stocks will effect this outcome? What are the odds that investing in bonds will do so? How about mutual funds? How about options?

We can research the historical performance of each investment type. While this research is no guarantee of future performance, it can help us to make reasonable estimates. It can inform us regarding the *probability* of specific outcomes, and thus aid us in deciding how to invest our money. Note how this mental model completely ignores the *possibility* of specific outcomes.

Time required: 40 minutes

TACTIC #13: PERFORM A PAIRED COMPARISON ANALYSIS

 Nothing is more difficult, and therefore more precious, than to be able to decide.

— Napoleon Bonaparte

W hen faced with a decision for which there are two options, we can use a number of tools to help us make the wisest, most productive choice. The preceding chapters have explored the most useful tools to that end. But how should we approach a decision for which we have several options, some related and others unrelated? How do we make the best possible choice?

Most of the tactics we've discussed in previous chapters

will help. But there's one tool that's specifically designed to aid us in this type of scenario: paired comparison analysis.

Paired comparison analysis gives us a way to consider a range of possibilities, systematically juxtaposing them against each other. It makes it possible to compare competing, disparate options where the appraisal criteria is subjective. In essence, this tool allows us to effectively compare apples to oranges in a way that leads to the right decision.

How Relativity Influences Our Decisions

We rarely, if ever, make decisions in a vacuum. Instead, we consider possible outcomes and evaluate them based on how they compare to one another. We weigh the risks associated with each outcome. We estimate the odds of each outcome's occurrence.

For example, suppose a friend confides in you "I know how you can grow your money by 15% a year." Given that the stock market has historically produced a 10% return each year, this claim sounds enticing. But you might reasonably pause and seek more information. More information allows you to compare your friend's promise to other options and weigh the attendant risks.

For instance, will you need to assume more risk to earn this higher potential return on your money? Will you need to tolerate more volatility? Will your money become inaccessible for a longer duration? Or suppose you operate your own business and currently enjoy a 25% return on your investment each year. How does your friend's promise measure up?

This is the concept of relativity in action. This is the context in which we normally make decisions. We evaluate options based on how they compare against each other.

For example, suppose you're offered a choice: receive $100 today or a greater amount at some point in the future. It's impossible to choose because you don't know the amount of money you'll receive in the future or how long you'll be required to wait to receive it. But let's say the choice is to either receive $100 today or $200 in six months. We can now compare these outcomes to one another and make a reasonable decision.

But let's complicate the matter. Suppose we're not limited to two possibilities. Suppose we have *four* options from which to choose.

A Simple Example of Paired Comparison Analysis

For this example, let's assume we're faced with the following choices:

Choice A: receive $100 today
Choice B: receive $200 in six months
Choice C: receive $125 in one week
Choice D: receive $1,000 in three years

These four choices are related in context, but otherwise disparate from one another. There's no clear link between them. The rate of return associated with each choice is different, and so our criteria for evaluating each must be subjective. How do we make the right decision?

First, we create a simple matrix. This matrix will allow us to rank each option against the others. You can do this on paper, but I recommend using a spreadsheet (Google Sheets is a good choice). A spreadsheet is easier to modify as needed.

List each option (Choices A through D) in the left-most column and along the top-most row of your matrix. Next, block out the redundant cells (color them grey). Here's how your matrix should appear:

OPTION	Choice A	Choice B	Choice C	Choice D
Choice A				
Choice B				
Choice C				
Choice D				

The next step is to establish our evaluation criteria. As noted above, this criteria will be subjective because our choices are unlinked by any quantitative measure. Following are two criteria we might use:

1. how much we desire the money
2. the urgency of our desire

Next, let's compare each option to the others using our subjective criteria. In each blank cell, enter the choice you prefer. Here's how your matrix might appear when you're done:

OPTION	Choice A	Choice B	Choice C	Choice D
Choice A		A	C	D
Choice B			C	D
Choice C				D
Choice D				

The final step is to count the number of times we selected each choice, and then rank the choices based on this tally. Following are the numbers ranked as prescribed:

Rank 1: Choice D (selected 3 times)
Rank 2: Choice C (selected 2 times)
Rank 3: Choice A (selected 1 time)
Rank 4: Choice B (unselected)

We can quickly see that Choice B performed miserably in comparison to the other options. We can also see that Choice D is the clear winner.

Note that this paired comparison analysis was a simple one. The decisions you face with multiple options available to you will often be more complex. Rest assured this tool will help you to make the right decision regardless of how many options you must compare against one another.

LET's put the above into (more) practice.

~

Exercise #13

~

THIS EXERCISE WILL REQUIRE a decision for which you have several options. A "binary" decision, such as whether or not you should buy a house, leave your job, or pursue an advanced degree, won't suffice. Paired comparison analysis is suited for situations where multiple options exist.

For example, suppose you run a business and have enjoyed a massive boost in sales this year. You now need to decide the best use for the resulting financial windfall. Following are some options:

- Pay down your business's debt
- Invest in capital equipment
- Give bonuses to your employees
- Execute a large advertising campaign
- Expand your sales team

The decision is complicated by the multiple potential courses of action. Paired comparison analysis will lead you to the right choice.

I'll demonstrate this exercise with a variant of our tried-and-true "invest $10,000" example. But as with Exercise #12 in the previous chapter, I encourage you to use a personal decision in its stead.

We have $10,000 and want to use the funds in a worthwhile manner. We have numerous options available to us:

1. Invest the money
2. Pay off high-interest credit cards
3. Buy a new car
4. Increase an emergency fund
5. Put in into a savings accounts
6. Start a business
7. Take a family vacation

These choices are unrelated. Consequently, there's no single objective gauge by which to measure and compare their respective merits. We need to come up with subjective criteria by which to appraise each of them. These criteria should reflect our priorities. For simplicity, let's assume we have only two criteria:

1. productive use of our money
2. level of time and effort required

The next step is to create a decision matrix. This matrix will comprise eight rows and eight columns to accommodate our seven options. Following is how it should appear:

OPTION	Choice 1	Choice 2	Choice 3	Choice 4	Choice 5	Choice 6	Choice 7
Choice 1							
Choice 2							
Choice 3							
Choice 4							
Choice 5							
Choice 6							
Choice 7							

Now, we'll compare each option (or choice) against one another and note the winners in the blank cells. For example, let's compare options 1 and 3 using our two subjective criteria:

1. Invest the money
3. Buy a new car

Option 1 accommodates our first criterion (productive use of our money). Option 3 does not, at least not to the same extent. With regard to our second criterion (level of time and effort required), both options are on equal footing. Both will require research.

In this case, Option 1 wins and should be so noted in the appropriate cell. After we perform these comparisons for all of our available options, our decision matrix may appear as follows:

OPTION	Choice 1	Choice 2	Choice 3	Choice 4	Choice 5	Choice 6	Choice 7
Choice 1		2	1	4	1	1	1
Choice 2			2	2	2	2	2
Choice 3				4	5	3	7
Choice 4					4	4	4
Choice 5						5	5
Choice 6							6
Choice 7							

Now, let's count the number of times each option "won." Following is the tally from the above matrix:

Choice 1: won 4 times
Choice 2: won 6 times
Choice 3: won 1 time
Choice 4: won 5 times
Choice 5: won 3 times
Choice 6: won 1 time
Choice 7: won 1 time

From this tally, we can see that Choice 2 (pay off our high-interest credit cards) is the clear winner based on our two criteria. Note that changes to these criteria will potentially alter your results.

Time required: 25 minutes

TACTIC #14: LET YOUR PERSONAL VALUES LEAD THE WAY

66 It's not hard to make decisions when you know what your values are.

— Roy E. Disney

Our decisions stem from our values even if we don't consciously think about them. For example, we decide to eat junk food because, at that particular moment, we value its taste and the sugar rush more than we value our health. We decide to nap because we value the benefits of napping (increased energy, improved mood, etc.) more than we value the benefits of other activities at that time.

As author Mark Manson once noted, "we do what we value."

We often make such decisions instinctively. For example, none of us performs a paired comparison analysis to decide whether to eat a donut, cupcake, or salad. We see it. We crave it. We eat it.

But that doesn't mean we can't use our personal values to make healthy, productive decisions in a thoughtful and methodical manner. The upside of doing so is, we'll act with confidence because our decisions will naturally align with our beliefs, convictions, and priorities.

Before we go further, let's define personal values.

Personal Values in a Nutshell

Our values define how we view the world around us. They determine what we find to be meaningful. They dictate what we consider to be ethical, virtuous, and important. They are the principles by which we assess the integrity of our actions, behaviors, and decisions. Our values are a major impetus in everything we do.

When we act in alignment with our personal values, we feel content. We experience a sense of satisfaction. Even when our decisions lead to unpleasant circumstances, we take solace when those decisions align with our values. Conversely, when we act counter to our principles, we feel at odds with ourselves. We experience a sense of discordance. Even if our decisions lead to stellar results, we feel disquieted and disappointed in ourselves.

The Value of Making Values-Based Decisions

Decisions are easier to make when they stem from our core values. Our values already inform our goals, prioritizing them according to what we consider to be meaningful and important. They can likewise be used to inform our choices toward achieving those goals.

For example, suppose you're thinking about quitting your job. While it's a high-paying job, it's also stressful and time-intensive. You normally work 65 to 70 hours per week, leaving you with little time or energy to do anything else.

Is quitting the right decision? Perhaps. Or perhaps not.

Let's say your values center around money. You prioritize building wealth above all other goals. Nothing is more important to you. In this case, quitting your job makes sense if you're pursuing a higher-paying job elsewhere. On the other hand, quitting to enjoy more free time would conflict with your values and leave you feeling dissatisfied.

Now, let's flip that perspective. Suppose you value time with your family above everything else. Money is nice, but pales in importance to spending quality time with your spouse and children. In *this* case, quitting your job to spend more time at home aligns with your values. If you decide to quit, you're more likely to feel satisfied with your decision, even if you make less money. Your decision is in harmony with your principles.

This is the reason it's important to let our personal values guide our decisions. It does no good to pursue optimal results if doing so means sacrificing our principles in the process.

Yes, we should seek out pertinent data when making decisions. We should weigh the practical pros and cons associated with our options. We should avoid cognitive biases and always challenge our assumptions. But ultimately, we should use our core values to appraise the merits of our choices. Only then can we experience the satisfaction that comes with acting in accordance with our fundamental beliefs, standards, and convictions.

Now let's determine what values should guide us in decision-making.

How to Create a Core List of Personal Values

Our personal values extend into various aspects of our lives. Some involve our behaviors. Examples include honesty, compassion, and kindness. Other values involve issues or causes that are important to us. Examples here might include community development, civic duty, and animal rights. Still other values involve our work-related lives. Examples can include accountability, efficiency, and hard work.

There are dozens of values we can - and arguably should - pursue in various areas of our lives (at home, at work, with friends, etc.). But it's important to identify a core set of five or six. This is a manageable number we can use to inform our choices without our become paralyzed by indecision.

To highlight this core set of values, start by exploring an exhaustive list. You can find many such lists online (search Google for "list of values"). Once you've found such a list, peruse it with a pen and pad of paper near you. Write down those that are particularly important to you. Limit your written list to 15 values.

Once you've finished perusing the exhaustive list, take a look at your written list. It's time to whittle it down to five or six *core* values. This may be a difficult task as every value you've written down is important to you. But it's a worthwhile endeavor to create a *manageable* list for practical use in our decision-making.

To trim your list, recall experiences upon which your listed values had a positive and consequential impact. Think about past decisions that made you feel satisfied and self-assured, even when the results were disappointing. Reflect on people you admire and the character traits they regularly demonstrate. Consider your high-priority goals and ask yourself why they're important to you.

By going through this process, you'll gradually pare down your written list of values to a manageable list of five or six. This will become your *core* list. These are the values you'll use to appraise whether your decisions align with what you consider to be meaningful and principled. These are the values that will ultimately allow you to feel confident in your choices.

LET's put the above into practice.

Exercise #14

This exercise is a quick and simple one. To complete it, you'll need your core list of personal values. If you have yet to create it as described above, I encourage you to do so now. I'll use the following list of personal values for illustrative purposes throughout this exercise:

- compassion
- dependability
- modesty
- fairness
- trustworthiness

First, think about an important decision you're currently facing or have recently grappled with. Write down all of your options.

Second, consider whether the decision itself is consistent with your core list. For example, suppose you've promised your family months ago that you'd take them on an expensive vacation during the summer. But with summer approaching, you're now tempted to severely trim the cost and spend the savings on yourself.

Review your core list of values. Does this decision align with them? Trimming the cost of the vacation may not necessarily violate your sense of compassion or modesty. But it *does* defy your sense of dependability and trustworthiness. It might also offend your sense of fairness. Based on these potential trespasses, you should dismiss the decision. Otherwise, it'll gnaw at your conscience.

Third, let's test our *options* against our core list of values. Let's suppose that you plan to take your family on a vacation, but the extent and cost of the vacation are still undecided. Keeping the cost down doesn't violate your values as no promise has been made regarding it. Following are a few options regarding what you might do with the resulting savings:

- Bolster your family's emergency fund
- Pay off your credit cards
- Repair the roof on your house
- Buy an expensive, flashy new watch
- Buy a new set of power tools

Measure the merit of each option against your core values. Ask yourself whether the option in question breaches any of them.

For example, using the savings to bolster your family's emergency fund is a responsible use of the funds. Paying off your credit cards can also be sensible. Repairing the roof on your house is arguably a prudent way to use the savings. On the other hand, buying an expensive, flashy new watch might violate your sense of modesty. And buying a new set of power tools might counter your sense of fairness (your family is unlikely to benefit from the purchase).

Here, our core list of values has helped us to whittle down our options, simplifying our decision. And importantly, it has left us with options with which we feel comfortable.

Time required: 15 minutes

PART III

HOW TO OPTIMIZE YOUR DECISION-MAKING RESULTS

~

We've arrived at the final section of this book. It's a short one. You already possess all the tools you need to make effective decisions that consistently produce good results. This section will provide additional insights to streamline the decision-making process.

For many people, making decisions is a constant struggle. We get distracted. We have difficulty choosing between options that seem equally appealing to us. We second-guess ourselves. Sometimes, we're presented with so many viable options that we become paralyzed with indecision. Other times, we become emotionally invested in the process. Plus, we're stressed out. We're anxious. And we're exhausted.

This section will ease the strain. We'll cover several

practical tips that'll help you to make smarter decisions faster. These tips encourage you to make confident choices without overthinking things.

Some of what follows will summarize points we've previously covered, but address them from a fresh perspective. The rest is comprised of mini insights you can use *immediately* to make decisions without fear or regret.

We'll end this section with a brief guide on how to create a feedback loop. Feedback loops are an integral, yet often overlooked, part of the decision-making process. They reveal whether our choices are effective, and encourage us to make adjustments that ultimately produce better outcomes down the road.

10 QUICK TIPS THAT'LL HELP YOU TO MAKE FASTER DECISIONS

> 66 Decision is a sharp knife that cuts clean and straight; indecision, a dull one that hacks and tears and leaves ragged edges behind it.

— GORDON GRAHAM

∾

The tips that follow have a single purpose, disparate as they might seem at first glance. They're designed to accelerate your decision-making.

Making faster decisions isn't *always* better than making slower ones, of course. Many decisions warrant contemplation and careful examination. But oftentimes, when we're faced with tough choices, we dawdle unnecessarily. This tendency may stem from fear, lack of confidence, emotional involvement, or simply having too much information in front of us. Whatever the case, these tips will help us to stay focused and make rational, effective decisions in half the time.

Tip #1: Give yourself a time limit

Working without a time limit opens the door to distraction. Without a deadline looming over us, we're tempted to set aside the matter at hand and pursue activities we find more immediately rewarding (for example, social media). We procrastinate.

Whenever you're faced with a decision, set a time limit. (For fast decisions, use the timer on your phone to keep you on track.) Make sure the time limit is reasonable, but aggressive, given the type of decision you're making.

For example, allow three minutes for inconsequential decisions (e.g. what to eat for dinner). Allot one or two hours for weightier matters (e.g. whether to start a particular side business). Devote a week or two to the truly important issues (e.g. whether to get married, seek a new job, or buy a new home).

The point is to create a deadline that encourages you to move forward without stalling.

Tip #2: Dismiss the trivial decisions

In *Part I: Understanding Our Decision-Making Process*, we noted the large volume of choices we make each day. Many of these choices are trivial despite seeming significant in the moment. For instance, recall that experts claim we make up to 200 decisions each day regarding food alone.

Just because we're faced with a decision doesn't mean it's worth mulling over. In fact, a large percentage of the decisions we spend time on aren't worth the time we spend on them. Here are a few examples from my own life:

- what to eat for lunch
- which type of horseradish sauce to buy
- which shirt to wear when I'm working from home
- whether to have the oil changed in my car today or tomorrow
- which grocery store to visit

And on and on. These choices seem important to me in the moment. But when I pull back the lens, they become trivial compared to other issues.

The best practice is to dismiss them. For example, when I visit the grocery store, I no longer ponder which type of horseradish sauce to buy. I grab one and move on. I'm not a horseradish sauce connoisseur, so the many options offer minimal value to me.

Tip #3: Simplify the decision as "good" or "bad"

Some decisions warrant our time and attention, but are neither pivotal nor urgent. We should consider them, but avoid overthinking them. One way to do this is to reframe our options as simply "good" or "bad."

Here, we're not interested in conducting a Go/No-Go Evaluation (Tactic #6), creating a weighted pros-and-cons list (Tactic #7), or performing a paired comparison analysis (Tactic #13). These less-consequential decisions hardly justify the effort. Instead, we appraise our options solely based on whether they're "good" or "bad."

For example, suppose you're contemplating which restaurant to visit for dinner: a new Mediterranean venue, a local diner, or a steakhouse. "Good" and "bad" will be defined by your mood, preferences, and circumstances (budget, available time, etc.). If you crave a steak, the steakhouse will probably win this battle. If you're in the mood to try a new place, the Mediterranean venue will likely win. If you're short on time, the local dinner will get your business.

Again, the point is to make these decisions quickly. Reframing options as simply "good" or "bad" based on our mood, preferences, and circumstances prevents us from obsessing over them.

Tip #4: Design for default

This term "choice architecture" was introduced by authors Richard Thaler and Cass Sunstein in their book *Nudge*. The premise is as follows: consumers' decisions are influenced by their environment. Businesses can improve consumers' decisions by creating an environment that minimizes biases.

One of the tools used toward this end is something called the "default effect." This effect describes the tendency for people to select the default option. This option is essentially chosen for us, dramatically reducing the mental effort required of us in selecting it.

Author James Clear argues that we can use this tool to improve our everyday decision-making. He calls the practice "designing for default."

Here's a simple example: suppose you're watching TV and suddenly crave a donut. You have no donuts in your home, so eating one entails driving to a donut shop. Meanwhile, your kitchen is filled with healthier snacks, such as almonds, yogurt, and apples. These options are your defaults. They are near you and easy to access.

By designing our environment with such defaults in mind, we can make faster decisions. And with forethought, these decisions will be healthier, more productive, and ultimately more effective for us.

For example, if we habitually carry a water bottle, we'll end up drinking water rather than a soda. If we turn off our phones during work sessions, we'll end up working rather than responding to texts, emails, and phone calls. If we refuse to keep sugary treats at home, we'll end up eating healthier snacks (or foregoing snacks altogether).

Design for default. Create an environment that essentially makes your decisions for you.

Tip #5: Accept that "good" may be good enough

Back in the 1950s, cognitive psychologist and Nobel Prize-winning economist Herbert A. Simon came up with a novel idea: satisficing.[1] The gist is that "good" is often good enough when making decisions. Optimal choices sometimes pale in comparison to sub-optimal choices by virtue of the fact that the former requires more resources (time, effort, capital, etc.). As long as our requirements are satisfied, a sub-optimal choice is arguably a good one. And "good" is often good enough.

For example, suppose we're deciding on purchasing a new car. Our requirements are simple. The car must be dependable, get good gas mileage, offer sufficient room, and come with select features (Bluetooth, heated seats, remote start, etc.). Many models satisfy these requirements. If we commit to the practice of satisficing, we'll quickly choose one from the bunch without obsessing about whether we're choosing the *best* option.

The upside of satisficing is that we'll make faster decisions with confidence. And as a bonus, according to Simon's research, we'll actually be *happier* with our decisions.

Tip #6: Rely on experienced-based intuition

Our intuition, on its own, is unreliable. Without raw experience to support it, intuition is little more than a gut feeling. And that's a mere step from guesswork, which makes it a questionable tool for decision-making.

Having said that, when our intuition is informed by experience, it becomes a highly-useful tool. One that we can depend upon to make fast, productive decisions with confidence.

According to William Duggan, professor at Columbia Business School and author of *Strategic Intuition: The Creative Spark in Human Achievement*, there are three types of intuition: ordinary intuition, expert intuition, and strategic intuition. Ordinary intuition is what we feel in our gut. Expert intuition is our recognition of familiar circumstances. This recognition stems from our experience. It allows us to quickly appraise the merits of disparate or conflicting courses of action.

Strategic intuition also stems from experience. But rather than helping us to act in *familiar* situations, it allows us to act in *unfamiliar* situations. When we're faced with a decision involving circumstances that are new to us, strategic intuition helps us to connect the dots and develop a viable strategy.

Previously, I advised against relying on our intuition when making important decisions. I stand by this advice, particularly as it regards *ordinary* intuition, or gut feeling. But when decisions involve issues that are familiar to us due to our experience, we can (and should) trust our intuition. We should depend on our *expert* intuition when making quick decisions. And we should depend on our *strategic* intuition when making decisions that require time, contemplation, and a procedural approach.

Tip #7: Apply the 10/10/10 rule

One of the most common stumbling blocks to effective decision-making is our emotional state. It's the reason behind the common advice to "sleep" on important decisions. Otherwise, we might choose rashly and later regret our choices.

Of course, a good night's rest isn't always sufficient to make rational, healthy decisions. It's possible to sleep well and still make regrettable choices the following day due to our emotional investment.

The 10/10/10 rule counters our tendency to invest ourselves emotionally in decisions. It does so by forcing us to examine how our choices will make us feel...

- in 10 minutes
- in 10 months
- in 10 years

Gauging our feelings in this way helps us to separate our emotions from our options. It gives us room to breathe and not obsess about the short-term ramifications of our choices.

For example, suppose you're deciding whether to take a long-needed vacation. You're stressed due to your job and desperately need a break. However, you're tempted to forego taking a vacation because of your job-related responsibilities. A small voice in the back of your head intimates that things will fall apart in your absence.

In this scenario, you're emotionally involved. Fear and anxiety are controlling the decision-making process. So ask yourself the following questions presuming that you've decided to take a vacation:

- How will I feel in 10 minutes?
- How will I feel in 10 months?
- How will I feel in 10 years?

In 10 minutes, you'll likely still feel panicky or anxious. This stems from your short-term emotional state.

In 10 months' time, you'll almost certainly be pleased that you took a break. The vacation will have lowered your stress, increased your productivity, improved your mood, and inspired your creativity.

In 10 *years'* time, you'll look back and chuckle at the predicament. In 10 years, you'll likely have advanced your career to the point that this past "dilemma" seems trivial to you. You may even have a different position, perhaps at a different company or organization.

The 10/10/10 rule can turn "difficult" decisions into easy ones by keeping our short-term emotions in check.

Tip #8: Avoid the Paradox of Choice

In the chapter *Tactic #10: Ignore the Sunk Cost Fallacy*, we discussed opportunity costs. In short, the resources we devote to one endeavor cannot be used to pursue other endeavors. These latter endeavors become the opportunity costs associated with our decisions.

The paradox of choice acknowledges this phenomenon as an obstacle to the decision-making process. The term was coined by psychologist Barry Schwartz in his book *The Paradox of Choice: Why More Is Less*. Schwartz notes that having a plethora of options initially appears to be an advantage. But paradoxically, this "advantage" becomes problematic when we're forced to choose one option from among the others. In fact, according to Schwartz, not only does this cause us anxiety, but after making our choice we inevitably experience regret due to the options we've foregone in the process.

For example, suppose you visit a grocery store to purchase a bottle of salad dressing. When you arrive, you're presented with dozens of options. Unsure of which one to select, you begin to feel anxious. Indecision sets in as you stand in the aisle staring at the fully-stocked shelves. Finally, you choose one. But following your decision, you begin to feel regret due to the tasty alternatives you're leaving behind (opportunity costs).

This is the paradox of choice. Having options equals freedom of choice, which is good. But having too many options leads to indecision, anxiety, paralysis, and ultimately regret.

One way to speed up our decision-making is to avoid this phenomenon altogether. When you're faced with a multitude of options, immediately ignore the majority of them and focus on the two or three most viable ones. Let's return to our hypothetical grocery store. Commit to ignoring 95% of the salad dressings on display. Instead, focus on the few you've enjoyed in the past. Select one and forget about the others. Quick decision, dependable results, and zero regret.

Tip #9: Reach for a lifeline

This is arguably the simplest tip of the bunch. It's also the one that's easiest to apply.

If you're having difficulty making a decision, ask someone for advice. Get another person's perspective. You might initially think that this individual needs to be knowledgeable, experienced, or intimately acquainted with the matter at hand. But this isn't always true.

According to Daniel Gilbert, author and professor of psychology at Harvard University, a randomly-chosen person can oftentimes provide helpful insight into how we might feel about a particular decision. This individual doesn't need to be like us. Nor does he or she need to have ever been in our particular situation. In his book *Stumbling on Happiness*, Gilbert argues that even randomly-chosen people can help us to predict how we'll feel about the outcomes of our decisions. Asking for their opinions can yield useful insight.

In short, if you're stuck, reach for a lifeline. Ask a friend or coworker for his or her opinion. If he or she has experience in the matter, great. If not, that's fine, too. You'll benefit either way.

Tip #10: Get comfortable with the possibility of failure

Success is never guaranteed. Even when we carefully investigate our options and meticulously apply the tactics covered in this book, there always exists uncertainty about the outcome. We can minimize the degree of uncertainty associated with our decisions, but we can rarely, if ever, eliminate it.

Left unchecked, this uncertainty inevitably leads to self-doubt and indecision. We take longer choosing between competing options because we're fearful of making choices that produce regrettable results. We begin to overthink situations. And so a decision that could be made quickly ends up taking far more time, effort, energy, and headspace than it warrants.

Here's a simple hack that'll help us to make faster decisions: get comfortable with the possibility of failure. Once we've done everything we can to minimize the chances of a poor outcome, we should simply forge ahead.

Bad outcomes happen, and sometimes there's no way to avoid them. Rather than overthinking a decision and becoming paralyzed by fear, we should accept that outcomes are ultimately uncertain. As long as we've taken reasonable steps to ensure *good* results (e.g. using the tactics in *Part II*), we should be willing to move forward despite the possibility of *bad* results.

THESE 10 TIPS are designed to help us make faster decisions with confidence. But note that none of them suggest we should act recklessly. On the contrary, we should still take the time to properly consider our circumstances, constraints, and goals. To this end, there are several questions we should ask ourselves to clarify what we hope to accomplish and ensure we maintain our focus and purpose.

We'll cover these questions in the next chapter...

---

1. https://en.wikipedia.org/wiki/Satisficing

10 QUESTIONS TO ASK YOURSELF BEFORE EVERY DECISION

 It is in your moments of decision that your destiny is shaped.

— TONY ROBBINS

Asking ourselves questions before we make decisions accomplishes two important aims. First, it disabuses us of impractical, idealistic notions. It forces us to focus on realistic goals and feasible options for bringing them to fruition.

Second, it reduces the anxiety that comes with decision-making. Answering these questions encourages us to become pragmatic about our emotions, goals, biases, values, and even the potential consequences associated with our choices. Addressing them upfront boosts our confidence. Our answers will either validate our reasoning, prompting us to move forward, or highlight issues that require more contemplation.

Brace yourself. We'll move quickly through these questions. You'll undoubtedly find some to be intuitive. A few others recall concepts we've discussed earlier but in a slightly different context. Either way, there's no reason to belabor them. But presenting them here in one place give you a "cheat sheet" of sorts that you can refer to whenever you're facing a tough decision.

Onward…

Question #1: What am I trying to achieve?

Sometimes, we become so mired in the minutiae of our decisions that we overlook the bigger picture. We can fix this problem with a few basic questions that highlight what we're trying to accomplish:

- What is my objective?
- What is my optimal outcome?
- Why am I doing this?
- For whom am I doing this?

(Yes, I turned this single question into four questions. All four are designed to answer the main one. It's productive because it encourages introspection and can lead to actionable insight. So fair warning: we'll be doing it again.)

Question #2: What will happen if I don't make this decision?

We often make decisions without considering whether we need to make them at all. Have you ever stopped to ask yourself:

- What happens if I *don't* make this decision?
- What regrets will I have if I simply do nothing?

You may find the answers to be illuminating. They might even prompt you to reevaluate whether a decision is necessary (saving you time, effort, and other resources in the process).

Question #3: How much risk am I able to tolerate?

As we've discussed, every decision is accompanied by uncertainty. Outcomes aren't entirely predictable regardless of how careful our investigation or exhaustive our analysis. This means we risk something every time we choose between competing options. Ask yourself:

- How much risk can I tolerate?
- Is the risk associated with a given option commensurate with the potential reward if things turn out as I anticipate?
- At what point does the level of risk become too burdensome?

Effective decision-making shouldn't be akin to playing roulette or baccarat in a casino. Every choice we make should be reasoned and practical, after weighing the potential consequences of a decision against its expected benefits.

Question #4: What personal biases are impairing my perspective?

We discussed common biases that obstruct our decision-making in the chapter *10 Cognitive Biases That Impact Our Decisions*. Here, we need to bring to light those with which we regularly struggle. Peruse that early chapter and while doing so ask yourself:

- Do I entertain any of these biases?
- How do they tend to influence my decisions?
- How might my perspective change if I ignored these biases?

Oftentimes, we make decisions without being aware of our personal biases. Asking and answering these questions pushes us to address them.

Question #5: How will I feel after making this decision?

The leading cause of regrettable decisions is our emotional state at the time of making them. Our visceral responses to our circumstances often prompt us to make choices that are clearly unwise given our long-term goals.

For example, we see a donut and immediately crave it. So we eat it knowing that doing so ruins our diet. Another example: we're physically attracted to someone we know to be a terrible match for us. But spurred by desire, we ask this person out on a date. In both cases, regret inevitably follows.

In the previous chapter, we discussed the 10/10/10 rule (Tip #7). We can use this tool to avoid making imprudent decisions prompted by our visceral reactions to stimuli and experiences. Recall that this tool requires that we ask ourselves:

- How will I feel in 10 minutes?
- How will I feel in 10 months?
- How will I feel in 10 years?

Doing so arrests our immediate emotions and impels us to consider our longer-term concerns. This alone can discourage us from pursuing rashly-made choices that lead to negative outcomes.

Question #6: What are the potential consequences of my decision?

Every decision carries consequences. When we fail to investigate them, we operate blindly. This leads to stress and anxiety, which in turn cause indecision. Or worse, we make decisions in a state of oblivion, unaware or uncaring that our choices have ramifications.

Both situations are problematic. The good news is, both can easily be avoided by asking yourself two simple questions before deciding on a course of action:

- What are the consequences of choosing this option?
- Are these consequences worth bearing to achieve my objective?

For example, suppose you intend to invest $10,000. One immediate consequence is that you won't be able to use that money to buy a new car. Given your goal of saving money, you're likely willing to tolerate this consequence.

These two simple questions increase our confidence in making decisions when we might otherwise hesitate.

Question #7: Will my decision align with my values?

We discussed the importance of making values-based decisions in the chapter *Tactic #14: Let Your Personal Values Lead the Way*. So I won't belabor those points here. Having said that, this topic is a useful waypoint as it encourages constructive questions that'll help us make choices we feel good about.

Before making an important decision, ask yourself:

- What are my core principles?
- Does this option align with these principles?
- How will I feel about myself if choose this option?

For example, suppose one of your core values is compassion. Now suppose an acquaintance has fallen on hard times and asks you to lend him money. You might initially balk at his request. But if making the loan aligns with your compassion, you may decide that doing so is the proper choice.

Question #8: How much time will I allow myself?

I love this question. It counters my tendency to overthink situations. Instead, it prompts me to take action when I might otherwise become unnecessarily mired in the details.

Prior to making a decision, ask yourself:

- How long will I allow myself to decide?

This question hearkens back to a topic we discussed in the chapter *Tactic #11: Identify and Avoid Information Overload*. There, we talked about the importance of setting time limits to avoid information overload (Step #4). Here, we use the same strategy to avoid indecision and procrastination.

By asking how much time you'll allow yourself, you can

set a reasonable deadline that applies helpful pressure. This deadline prevents you from needlessly postponing making the decision.

Question #9: How would I counsel someone else in my situation?

Imagine that someone else is struggling with the decision you're facing. This person asks your advice. What would you tell him or her?

This exercise is useful because it's easier to advise someone regarding *their* options than it is to make such choices for ourselves. The reason is because we feel a degree of detachment. We're not emotionally involved with the matter. Because our mind isn't clouded by our emotions, we can more easily make rational decisions.

So if you're struggling with a tough decision, ask yourself:

- How would I advise someone else in my predicament?

This question can strip away our visceral reactions to our circumstances. In doing so, it can help us to make reasoned, productive decisions based on data rather than our short-term emotional state.

And that neatly brings us to our final question…

Question #10: How is my current emotional state influencing my perspective?

We've talked a great deal about the role of emotion in decision-making throughout this book. Our emotions can be both a stumbling block and an aid depending on the circumstances. They can trigger our biases and cause indecision or spur us to investigate matters that are important to us.

For this reason, before making any important decision, it's useful to ask yourself:

- What emotions am I feeling at this moment?
- How are these emotions influencing my decision?

Asking these two questions forces us to acknowledge our immediate emotional state and assess whether it's helping or hindering our ability to make a good decision. Do we feel irritated, fearful, or hostile? Or do we feel inspired, confident, and optimistic? These emotions can have a huge impact on us. Left unexamined and unchecked they can play a pivotal role in our decisions, for better or worse.

Most of the questions above are simple ones. You can answer them in moments. But don't underestimate their value. You'll find that they broaden your awareness about your thinking in ways that improve and accelerate your decision-making.

We now arrive at the final chapter of this book. It's a relatively short one, but covers a subject that is crucial to improving our decision-making skills over the long run.

HOW TO CREATE A FEEDBACK LOOP

66 Your emotions are making it difficult to accept hard decisions.

—JOHN C. MAXWELL

F eedback loops are present in every aspect of our lives. We find them in our workplaces, in our homes, and on social media. They're present when we interact with friends, family members, clients, and service personnel. They are ubiquitous even if we fail to immediately recognize them.

Sometimes, these feedback loops are designed with a specific purpose. For example, businesses often create them as a way to measure performance. Other times, they evolve organically as we learn the positive and negative effects of our behaviors. This is often the case with how we interact with our friends and loved ones.

We can create feedback loops that serve a similar purpose when it comes to making decisions. These loops will help us appraise our decisions based on their respective effects and make adjustments to our process when necessary or beneficial.

For example, imagine that you're playing a game of chess. Each move you make results in feedback as your opponent takes his or her turn. This feedback reveals whether your previous move advanced your position or impeded it. At the end of the game, you can review your performance in light of this feedback and adjust your approach for better results in the future. This is a simple feedback loop in practice.

Below, we'll explore the two main types of feedback loops. We'll then create one that we can use to evaluate our decisions and ultimately improve our decision-making skills.

Two Types of Feedback Loops

Feedback loops come in two varieties: reinforcing loops and balancing loops. Both are useful.

Reinforcing feedback loops are also known as positive loops. They "reinforce" and amplify the effects of existing systems. For example, suppose you deposit $1,000 into a bank savings account. This sum earns interest. The earned interest is added to the account, resulting in a greater sum.

Interest is then earned on this new, larger sum. Compound interest is an example of a reinforcing, or positive, feedback loop.

Balancing feedback loops are often referred to as *negative* loops. They counter the effects of existing systems. For example, consider the thermostat that controls your air conditioning unit at home. On hot days, when the gauge reaches a predetermined point, the unit turns on to cool your home. When the resulting temperature decreases to another predetermined point, the unit turns off. The thermostat is an example of a balancing, or negative, feedback loop.

With the above in mind, let's create a simple feedback loop that'll improve our decision-making prowess.

4 Steps to Creating an Effective Feedback Loop

THERE'S no need to overcomplicate this process. Every feedback loop is comprised of four basic steps (and the fourth one often requires no action):

1. data collection
2. data analysis
3. data assessment
4. course correction

Let's quickly break down each one.

Step #1: Collect Post-decision Data

All decisions impose effects. This step focuses on gathering information regarding these effects.

For example, suppose we've started a strength training workout routine. Some of the effects of this routine are changes in our weight, body composition (fat vs. muscle), and the amount of weight we're able to lift.

In order to know whether the routine we've chosen is producing our expected results, we must collect this data to analyze later. To streamline this process, we might keep a workout journal in which we record these metrics on a daily or weekly basis.

Step #2: Analyze the Data

Once we've collected the data stemming from our decision, we need to review it. Here, we're not interested in turning the data into meaningful insights. We merely want to organize it in such a way that we'll be able to measure our results against our expectations in Step #3.

In the case of our strength training example, we might calculate the amount of weight we've lost over the past 30 days. We may also record our week-by-week body composition ratios. And we'll want to document the weekly increase in the amount of weight we're able to lift.

We can easily determine these figures from the metrics we've kept in our workout journal. Once we've calculated them, it's time to compare them against our projections.

Step #3: Measure the Results against Your Expectations

Whenever we make a decision, we do so with an outcome in mind. We know intuitively that outcomes are uncertain. But if we approach decisions methodically, investigating all of our options and using relevant, fact-based information to choose wisely from among them, we can confidently anticipate the results.

This step is where we test our *actual* results against our *anticipated* results. If they match, it's an indication that our early decisions were on target. If they diverge, especially by a large margin, the variance indicates that our early decisions were impractical given our expectations.

For our strength training example, we might start our self-prescribed workout routine with the following expectations after 30 days:

- lose 8 lbs.
- reduce body fat percentage to 21%
- bench press an increase of 25 lbs.

Compare these expected results with the numbers we've calculated from the metrics in our workout journal (i.e. our *actual* results). If the figures match, terrific! If they don't match, we may need to make adjustments to our workout routine. Along the way, we learn to make better decisions in this area.

Step #4: Consider Possible Course Corrections

The purpose of course corrections is to improve the results we experience from similar decisions we make in the future. Making corrections closes the feedback loop (although the loop reopens at the start of the next decision).

For example, suppose after 30 days our strength training workout routine resulted in the following:

- We lost 6 lbs.
- We reduced our body fat percentage to 25%
- We increased the amount we are able to lift by 20 lbs.

These are positive results, but they fail to match our expectations. So we should return to our initial decisions (e.g. our creation of the routine) and figure out the reason(s) for the discrepancies.

Perhaps we should add another day of strength training to our weekly regimen (e.g. work out four days per week instead of three). Maybe we should perform high-intensity interval training two days each week instead of one. Perhaps we should increase the number of sets and repetitions we do for bench presses.

Note how this feedback loop uses our results to highlight shortcomings in our early decisions - in this case, the initial workout routine we created. And importantly, it encourages us to make adjustments that should yield better results down the road. Again, this process helps us to become more knowledgeable and more skilled in making these types of decisions.

How to Optimize Your Decision-Making Feedback Loop

We need two basic elements to ensure our feedback loop does its job:

1. a method for tracking data
2. the ability to analyze and measure data quickly

The method we use for tracking data can be as simple as the workout journal in our strength training example. There, we wrote down our body weight, body fat percentage, and the amount of weight we lifted each day. Of course, our tracking system can be far more complex depending on the types of decisions we face.

For example, if we've decided to adopt a new diet, we can use a variety of apps to keep track of the relevant daily metrics (nutritional values of meals, calories, etc.). In a business setting, we might use daily status reports, automated customer surveys, and similar tools. The important thing is to have such a system in place.

The ability to analyze and measure data quickly is equally important. The more time that passes between our decisions and our assessment of the results, the less influence those results will have on our future decisions.

For example, suppose we start our hypothetical strength

training workout routine on January 1st. We've listed our 30-day expectations with regard to weight loss, reduction in body fat percentage, and amount of weight we're able to lift. Each day, we dutifully record the relevant metrics in our workout journal.

Let's further suppose that we neglect to *analyze* our metrics and compare our 30-day results with our expected results. Six months pass. We still haven't determined whether our decisions regarding our original workout routine were successful. Consequently, we've made no course corrections. The metrics we tracked during the first 30 days have lost relevance and will ultimately have minimal influence on our ability to make wise decisions in this area in the future.

Feedback loops play a pivotal role in improving our decision-making aptitude. They help us to review our choices, evaluate their efficacy, and make changes when doing so is beneficial to us. But our feedback loops are only as effective as our ability to make use of the information they're designed to track. To that end, we need a reliable method for tracking it along with the means to analyze it in a timely manner.

FINAL THOUGHTS ON HOW TO MAKE BETTER DECISIONS

~

Tragedies and strokes of luck aside, we are the authors of our lives. Our successes and failures, joys and regrets, in practically every circumstance stem from our decisions. The more effective we are at making rational, healthy, productive decisions, the better results we enjoy.

Indeed, the better we become at making good decisions, the greater our quality of life will become over the long run. Our careers will advance. Our relationships will improve. Our finances will grow stronger. And with these core areas of our lives on solid ground, our outlook will naturally become more positive and our happiness will swell. We'll take greater pleasure in our interests and hobbies, knowing that we've made choices that not only propel us toward success, but also align with our values.

Such is the long-term effect of making good decisions.

But none of us is born with this skill. We learn it through trial and error. While it's possible to glean insights into the decision-making process by reading books and observing others, true growth in this crucial skill can only come via experience.

How to Make Better Decisions gives you the tools you need to master this area of your life. Its purpose is twofold: to help you learn the art of effective decision-making and provide practical exercises that encourage you to put this knowledge to use.

Most people want to make good decisions on a consistent basis. Many will even seek tips and guides on how to do so. But far fewer will actually take steps to develop this skill. They might start reading a book on decision-making (perhaps even this one), but grow bored with it and eventually abandon it.

You're clearly cut from a different fabric. You've finished reading *How to Make Better Decisions* and hopefully completed the exercises. You've already advanced further than most down the path toward becoming proficient at decision-making. Congratulations! You've made an investment in yourself that's guaranteed to produce dividends throughout your life.

DID YOU ENJOY READING HOW TO MAKE BETTER DECISIONS?

∼

This book is longer than most of my others. And although it's information-dense and chock-full of practical exercises, it's not a "sexy" read. No doubt reading the latest James Patterson or Nora Roberts novel is more fun.

For this reason, I'd like to thank you for taking the time to read *How to Make Better Decisions*. I hope you've found the experience enjoyable and the advice and tools useful. And I truly hope the tips, hacks, and exercises described in detail throughout this book will have a positive, long-term impact on your quality of life.

I now have a small favor to ask you.

If you enjoyed reading this book, would you please take a moment and leave a review on Amazon? Reviews are a *tremendous* help for independent authors like myself. They encourage other folks to read my books. Your words will go a long way toward persuading them.

One last note... if you'd like to be notified when I release new books (typically at a steep discount), I encourage you to sign up for my mailing list at:

http://artofproductivity.com/free-gift/

You'll receive immediate access to my 40-page PDF guide *Catapult Your Productivity: The Top 10 Habits You Must Develop to Get More Things Done.* You'll also receive actionable advice on beating procrastination, creating morning routines, avoiding burnout, developing razor-sharp focus, and more!

If you have questions or would like to share how you made a decision that improved your life in some way, please feel free to reach out to me at damon@artofproductivity.com. I'd love to hear from you!

UNTIL NEXT TIME,

Damon Zahariades
http://artofproductivity.com

ABOUT THE AUTHOR

Damon Zahariades is a corporate refugee who endured years of unnecessary meetings, drive-by chats with coworkers, and a distraction-laden work environment before striking out on his own. Today, in addition to being the author of a growing catalog of time management and productivity books, he's the showrunner for the productivity blog ArtofProductivity.com.

In his spare time, he enjoys playing chess, poker, and the occasional video game with friends. And he continues to promise himself that he'll start playing the guitar again.

Damon lives in Southern California with his beautiful, supportive wife and their affectionate, quirky, and sometimes mischievous dog. He's looking wistfully at his 50th birthday in the rearview mirror.

OTHER BOOKS BY DAMON ZAHARIADES

The Mental Toughness Handbook

The definitive, step-by-step guide to developing mental toughness! Exercises included!

To-Do List Formula

Finally! Discover how to create to-do lists that work!

The Art Of Saying NO

Are you fed up with people taking you for granted? Learn how to set boundaries, stand your ground, and inspire others' respect in the process!

The Procrastination Cure

Discover how to take quick action, make fast decisions, and finally overcome your inner procrastinator!

Fast Focus

Here's a proven system that'll help you to ignore distractions, develop laser-sharp focus, and skyrocket your productivity!

The 30-Day Productivity Plan

Need a daily action plan to boost your productivity? This 30-

day guide is the solution to your time management woes!

The 30-Day Productivity Plan - VOLUME II

30 MORE bad habits that are sabotaging your time management - and how to overcome them one day at a time!

The Time Chunking Method

It's one of the most popular time management strategies used today. Triple your productivity with this easy 10-step system.

80/20 Your Life!

Achieve more, create more, and enjoy more success. How to get more done with less effort and change your life in the process!

Small Habits Revolution

Change your habits to transform your life. Use this simple, effective strategy for adopting any new habit you desire!

Morning Makeover

Imagine waking up excited, energized, and full of self-confidence. Here's how to create morning routines that lead to explosive success!

The Joy Of Imperfection

Finally beat perfectionism, silence your inner critic, and overcome your fear of failure!

The P.R.I.M.E.R. Goal Setting Method

An elegant 6-step system for achieving extraordinary results in every area of your life!

Digital Detox

Disconnect to reconnect. Discover how to unplug and enjoy a more mindful, meaningful, and rewarding life!

For a complete list, please visit

http://artofproductivity.com/my-books/

Printed in Great Britain
by Amazon

67111013R00142